A DARK RIDE

A DARK RIDE

A Castle Family Adventure

Rebecca Jones

CHRISTIAN FOCUS PUBLICATIONS

© 1995 Rebecca Jones
ISBN 1-85792-130-5

Published by
Christian Focus Publications Ltd
Geanies House, Fearn, Ross-shire,
IV20 1TW, Scotland, Great Britain

Cover design by Donna Macleod
Cover illustration by Pete Roberts,
Allied Artists

Printed and bound in Great Britain by
Cox & Wyman Ltd, Reading, Berks

Contents

1

LEFT IN THE DUST

Fanny Castle turned sixteen at 10:20 a.m. on May 15th, the very moment a taxi rushed her mother to the hospital. The fifth Castle child was in a hurry to join his two sisters and two brothers. Dust blew into Fanny's eyes as the taxi roared up the gravelly driveway. Her mother's voice still floated in the southern French sunshine. 'Keep your eye on Nicky. He's only three.'

'Don't worry, mom,' she had answered. 'The kids will be fine 'til Madame Didier comes tomorrow.' But now Fanny's brave smile faded. Dad was on another business trip to Germany and it couldn't be helped: she was in charge for the night.

She felt small, standing alone on the valley floor. The stillness was suffocating. The scruffy valley walls stifled a rooster's late cry to the wide sky of Provence. Fanny glanced across the field to 'grouchy Griffon's' house, hoping to find some comfort in the presence of the neighbour. But a clang of tools grated against the silence. Naked metal car bodies lay in the junk-strewn field. Seven twisted cars on the left. Seven sleek cars on the right. 'Happy birthday, sweetie!' their grinning bumpers seemed to say, mocking cruelly. Her brother Max claimed Griffon was a car thief. A cut and paster, Max called him. She could just about believe it today. A red van stood ready to swallow each sleek car and carry it away at midnight. Fanny imagined it swallowing her, and shivered in spite of the sun.

She turned to her family's pink stucco house. The two wings on the ground floor seemed like arms, stretching wide to welcome her. 'It's no big deal,' she said out loud to herself. 'A night in your own home.'

She opened the heavy front door with a sigh of relief, and walked into the cool hallway. But as she turned to close it, the door resisted her pressure. Someone was pushing it open from the outside. Ordinarily, Fanny would have opened the door, afraid to trap Nicky or Caroline. But they were at school. Fear urged her to push it closed. She shoved at it, but whoever was on the outside flung it open suddenly and hard, knocking Fanny off her feet and over the landing step into the living room. She cried out with pain, and looked up. There stood Monsieur Griffon, square, ugly, and angry. Over his arm hung the same shotgun he had used to frighten the mailman. The story had seemed funny the day Max had told the family about it at the dinner table. Now Fanny cringed against the wall under the bar.

'*Sale gamine!*' he raged. 'You think I don't know

your brother spies on me all day? Little thief, he is. Walked off with the roof from one of my cars.'

Griffon toyed with the gun as he yelled. 'You kids stay off my property, you hear? And tell that nosy mother of yours to stay away from my wife. Puttin' ideas into her head. Sees her on the sly at the post office.'

Griffon took a step closer to Fanny. But he didn't see the step down from the entry landing. He stumbled and fell, the shotgun skidding across the floor. In bounded a large, black labrador. But instead of attacking Fanny, it stood in front of her, as if to protect her from Griffon, whose fall had made him angrier than ever. He grabbed his shotgun and stalked out, hurling more bad language at Fanny in three seconds than she had heard in her whole life.

The dog seemed anxious to stay, but Griffon returned to kick him viciously through the door. Fanny, shaking, hitched herself close to the door and closed it. She sat with her back against it for a long time before she got up, locked it, and made herself a cup of strong, black coffee. She supposed she should call the police, but she would wait for Max to come home. He would know what to do. Meanwhile, she had a lot to do before walking to school for Caroline and Nicky.

She scrubbed and cleaned as fast as her heart bumped. It helped her get her anger out. Imagine frightening someone like that. She was glad Nicky had not been there, though she would feel less lonely right now with him on her knee, his soft, silky hair against

9

her cheek as she read him the *Stubborn Rhinoceros* book. Nicky was in pre-school. She would walk to the village to get him and Carrie soon. The thought frightened her now. Would Griffon be watching? Would he come again?

Fanny plunged into housework. Nine year old Caroline's bed was a disaster. Tugging hard at the top sheet, Fanny sighed in disgust. "Being sweet isn't everything, Miss Caroline Castle," she thought, mentally lecturing her younger sister. Fanny stuffed a pile of messy books into the closet and tackled the desk. Paper clips, pencil shavings, empty ink-cartridges and bits of stickers were everywhere. "What's more," thought Fanny, "nobody scolds little Carrie." Her eyes fell on a drawing pad. The page was covered with paws, heads, tails, and sketches of eyes and ears. All monkeys. All very good. She slung the pad under Caroline's bed. Let her clean up her own mess. As she did, she noticed a little white jewellery box just like the box of earrings she had lost. She sat down on the bed to open it. There were her favourite earrings, turquoise shell on a silver background. Rachel had bought them for her in Mexico.

"Why the little sneak!" thought Fanny. 'I knew it,' she said out loud. She had been convinced for a long time that Caroline stole things. Nobody had wanted to believe her. Now she had evidence. She would have a word with her on the way home from school. But the thought of going out set her heart thumping. She put the earrings back in her own room, glancing out the window nervously.

Now for Max's room. Fanny thought Peter Maximilian Castle, fourteen, a little too smart for his own good. But she admired him. At school they called him Pierre. There wasn't much to do in Max's room. He spent all his time outside, reading or building forts. Fanny wrinkled her short nose as she entered the room. 'Yuk, those horrible socks!' she exclaimed, then clapped her mouth shut, half expecting Griffon to appear again. Fanny reached up to the windows, wishing she could throw them wide open to let in the breeze with its close, fragrant odour of thyme. The sky was so blue, the sun so bright. The majestic Sainte Victoire mountain lay shimmering, hazy, behind the hillside. Each day, each hour it looked different, yet always solidly the same. A bit like God, she had often thought. But today it shrank away from her, infinitely far away.

"The chicken!" she remembered, and ran for the freezer.

2

HOME, SWEET HOME

'Hi, Fanny! What're you doing home?' asked Max, flinging his book bag down on the living room floor.

'Any tea? Where's Mom?'

'No tea unless you make it yourself. Mom's in the clinic. The baby's on the way. And go put that bag away this minute. I've had to stay home all day on my birthday, and clean up, make the supper, get the kids, and ...'

Wow. He had never seen good old Fanny in such a state!

'Max! I've been waiting for hours!' Caroline burst into the room with Nicky, who was hanging off the back of her blue sweat shirt, dragging his feet along the floor and giggling.

'Fanny says I can't go bird-watching, just because I borrowed her earrings and forgot to put them back.'

'Can't you take me instead? She's all worried about grouchy Griffon, but you're not scared. If I don't go now, I won't get my report in on time!'

'Hang on a minute, Caroline,' protested Max, as he flopped into a chair with a puff of frustration. 'I just want a cup of tea! Let me think straight.'

'Me too, me too!' shouted Nicky. 'I wanna see the birds! CHEE! CHEE! CHEE!' With every 'chee' he tugged harder on Caroline's clothes.

'Let go, Nicky!' yelled Caroline. 'You can't come... you have to have your bath,' she added, pleased to find an excuse. Nicky began to howl and Fanny dropped an egg on the floor.

'Shut up, and get out, all of you. How can I get supper if you're all in here arguing and fighting?'

'Oh, stop playing mom,' scowled Max, running his fingers through his hair. 'It doesn't matter what we eat. Let's take what we want. It'll be easier for you that way.'

'It's all planned,' Fanny countered. 'Supper will be ready at seven o'clock. But I want to talk to you in the bedroom, Max.'

Maybe it was Fanny's preachy tone. Maybe it was the disappointment of having no tea. Maybe he was cross with himself for not remembering her birthday.

'That's what *you* have planned,' Max retorted, suddenly angry. 'How 'bout *me*? You tell me to get out and now you want to talk to me. Give me a sermon, I guess. Well you can talk to yourself about your plans!' Caroline's bottom lip slid out as her dreams for a bird-walk disappeared. Nicky kept on chirping.

'NICKY!!! BE QUIET!!' Max roared, jumping out of the chair and shaking poor little Nicky, whose eyes opened wide in surprise. As soon as Max let go, the little boy dashed into the kitchen, finding safety behind Fanny's kneeling figure, but knocking her off balance into the broken egg, which she was scraping up.

'Tell him to take me, Fanny,' pleaded Caroline hopelessly. 'And Nicky can't come. He'd ruin everything.'

Fanny rubbed harder at the slime with a sponge. 'Doesn't *anybody* know where the binoculars are?' pleaded Caroline.

'You're *not* going on a bird-walk, Caroline, and that's final.'

Suddenly Nicky screamed, a tight little sound. Fanny's stomach knotted. She dashed over to the stove, where Nicky was hopping up and down in pain. On his finger was an enormous blister where he had obviously touched the burner.

'Now look what's happened!' shouted Fanny. 'Get out of here, you two! Get out! Get out! Get out!! If you hadn't been in here fighting, Nicky wouldn't be hurt!'

Max stomped furiously out the front door. 'What a judgmental prig!' he thought. He hadn't even been in the kitchen. Oh, he would get out all right, but he would not be bossed around by a know-it-all, goody-goody sister who was, after all, only a year and a half older than he was, and in the same grade in school. He snatched a screw driver, hinge and spring which he had laid out in the garage before school, stuffed them into the side bag of his mo-ped, jumped on, and rode off up the hill. Caroline wouldn't dare pester him today.

There was no one around to whom she could tattle if he threatened her with any cruel and unusual treatment for getting near his secrets. Not that he intended to use any of them, but she was easy to scare.

He leaned the mo-ped against the bank of earth near his hideaway, pushed through the door, which was waiting for its home-made automatic hinge, and sat down in the old easy chair he had found on a nearby dump. It was comfortable now that he had re-done the cushion with foam rubber. The roof of his hut was a real treasure - a hood from one of Griffon's abandoned cars. He'd had the idea one night last summer after a midnight swim. It had been heavy, and awkward in the dark, but he'd managed it somehow. Max wondered if the grouch had been looking for it. "Serve him right for the way he treats that dog," he thought, and smiled grimly. He pulled himself out of his seat with a sigh.

Why couldn't Fanny treat him as an equal, instead of having to lord it over him to prove some kind of silly authority? She was so judgmental and defensive. Couldn't she just relax and live? "If she'd been nice to me," he reasoned, "I wouldn't have given her any trouble."

His eyes fell on the picnic box, and he thought of the binoculars hidden inside.

'Oh, darn,' he muttered. 'Caroline's looking for them. I'll have to sneak them back inside tonight.'

3

THE BIRD WALK

Caroline had watched Fanny read the medical guide to see what to put on Nicky's burn. Then she had found the cream, gauze, tape, and scissors. Now Nicky was upstairs in the bathroom. Fanny was scrubbing his freckled face and had promised him a tape before getting him into his pyjamas. A bath was out of the question. Caroline was determined to escape. Fanny had told her to get out. She would. It didn't matter if Max wasn't with her. Great galumphing Max would spoil a bird-walk anyway.

She had slipped her camera into her jeans' pocket while looking for the gauze. Now she tucked her sketch pad and pencils close to her side, hoping Fanny would not come back through the living room.

Caroline slipped noiselessly through the open front door. Outside, she walked around the west end of the house, which had no windows. Stepping on the lawn rather than the gravel paths, she made her way into the bushes. Caroline was not afraid of the neighbour.

Today she felt even more courageous, because she was so angry with Fanny. She would get back at Fanny for calling her a thief. She would prove she could go on a silly bird-walk without the neighbour murdering her!

Striking across the hillside she came to the ruin of the shepherd's hut. She peeked in. Only a tumble of rocks. Settling onto a warm stone, she set her sketch pad and pencils down and touched her pocket. The camera was still there. No need to get it out just yet; she might leave it behind. Mom didn't want her on the Griffon property, but she could only find birds where there were trees and these were the only ones the forest fire had spared. She leaned against the dusty stone wall and looked out of the 'window' of the hut. The sky was so blue it seemed thick. Sharp needles of irregular pines scratched at that blue, hoping to pull off a layer. Caroline thought of brooms, of dead pine needles and sparkling fires. She watched the dark, patchy bark. What birds lived here? She had only seen pigeons, magpies, and an occasional sparrow.

Last winter a European robin with a washed-out orange bib had hopped onto the window ledge, a sign of snow. Sure enough, there had been a blizzard, rare in Provence. That day the car couldn't climb the steep driveway. They had spent a heavenly morning making snowmen. The only black spot on that day was losing Fanny's best ring in the snow. She had only borrowed it for dressing up.

A stringy, red squirrel scampered up the tree, bringing her back to the present. It looked straight at her, twitching a nervous tail, as if frightened and trying to warn her. Looking right and left, around and behind, it dashed back down the tree. Caroline only laughed and shifted position to take up watch again.

The sun crept closer to the roof of Monsieur Griffon's untidy house. But it would take some time before Caroline would see one of those glorious sunsets that set the whole valley aglow. Their blaze was only surpassed by that of the fires. The fires brought terror, but the sunset brought only peace. She glanced at her watch. Nearly half past six. In only a half hour Fanny would call for supper. She must see some birds.

The warmth of the westering sun on her back made her feel as if the rays had gone right into her heart and were seeping out of her into the stone of the wall. How she loved to be outside alone.

Where was Mom right now? Was the baby born? What was it like to have a baby? She remembered the day Nicky came home; his funny grimaces, and snuffly noises. How attracted yet fearful she had been. Only five at the time, she had sat beside him for hours while he slept, watching him, singing, touching his soft head. She had changed diapers, helped him walk, read to him, and played with him. Now Nicky would have only Caroline put him to bed, even when Mommy was there. She thought of his burnt hand and felt uneasy at having left him. But she *did* have her bird report to do. And Fanny loved Nicky too.

The brief disturbance in her soul sailed off, dispersing like wisps of cloud. Caroline closed her eyes and listened. The only sound she could hear was a living lull that reminded her she was outside and not in. There were no voices, no animals, no machines, no passing cars - and *no* birds! Only throbbing fragrance. Only the tender sunlight creeping away with her thoughts, leaving her empty and warm. Caroline fell asleep.

4

BINOCULARS

Max picked the binoculars out of the picnic box. Looking down to the house below, he saw a flat-faced woman scrubbing a heavy black pot at the kitchen sink. Was she dreaming as she worked, Max wondered? Did she wish she could be on the hillside reading a book? What did she know about the field full of cars, or the car full of unshaven, foreign-looking men Max had seen coming down the driveway at midnight last Saturday?

The binoculars roamed over the fields, high with grass and weeds, tinged blood-red with poppies. He examined the swimming pool, if such a green, slimy, overgrown mess was still worthy of such a name. The mysterious blue tent to the side of the pool had to be a garage, Max decided. It could hold about four cars. Several men came out of a door flap. Carrying tools, they chatted and laughed as they crossed the untidy lawn to the main house and pushed at the bell. The worn front door opened and Max saw Monsieur

Griffon's face. It seemed to have slipped down his skull, pulling his eyebrows together into a great bush that threatened to swallow his eyes. His flat nose was too close to his upper lip, and jowls sagged onto his red neck. He was a squat-looking man, mean and humourless.

Max had met the neighbour when he came to recover his dog. The dog was nice, but Monsieur Griffon... Max shuddered as he remembered the man's violent blows with a metal bar, and the callous jerk with which he had thrown the dog into the back of his Peugeot. Why did he only like Peugeots, and like them enough to have a field full of them?

Max chewed unconsciously at his cheek as he watched the two men below talking animatedly with Monsieur Griffon, whose deep frown was alarming. But the two mechanics, as Max supposed them to be, continued their conversation undaunted, punctuating each statement with flailing movements. It was amazing that they did each other no harm, for each clung to his heavy tools.

He tired of watching them and turned his gaze to the hills around. Most of the driveway across the valley was in view, and all of the hillside opposite. In his sights now was the shepherd's hut at the edge of the field. Caroline wanted it for a hideout, but mom was afraid of the hunters, and dad didn't want her on the Griffon property. As Max watched, he thought he saw a flash of blue behind the wall. He looked again, keeping the binoculars very still. Nothing. That was the colour of Caroline's sweat shirt, he mused. Surely she hadn't set up to watch birds in the neighbour's hut? Max watched the spot where he had seen the flash of colour. Of course if Caroline was bird-watching, she would be very still. She was a patient little girl.

Seeing no further hint of movement, he turned the binoculars back to the house. Through the kitchen window Max saw the young flat-faced woman who, he supposed, had the unwanted honour of being married to Monsieur Griffon. She was still scrubbing heartlessly at the black pot. As Max watched, she looked over her shoulder into the room behind her. Then she dropped the pot hastily and backed up against the sink, wiping her hands nervously on her apron. Into Max's sights moved Monsieur Griffon, waving a paper and shouting soundlessly. Like a silent movie the scene played out in front of him. The young lady protesting, defending. Monsieur Griffon bearing down on her, jabbing a thick finger at the paper. Wisps of damp, dirty hair falling onto the woman's mended cardigan. The paper floating to the floor, trampled. The man shaking her. Her head waggling this way and that. His hand up. A blow. The woman sliding to the floor. Griffon stomping out of his kitchen, kicking the woman's bare foot out of his way.

Max felt his blood run cold. The binoculars pressed into his eyebrows, but he had squeezed his eyes shut, tight shut. All was absurdly still.

5

IT'S NICKY

Fanny settled Nicky onto the couch to listen to his 'monster' tape and wondered where Caroline had gone. The chicken smelled encouraging. But Nicky's catastrophe and Max's stormy arrival had prevented her from even starting the rice. Of course there would be no birthday cake. It was six-forty and she'd promised supper for seven. She only hoped Max had the sense to stay away from the Griffon's. He'd stomped off angry before she'd even had the chance to warn him.

"At least Nicky's quiet," she thought, as she poured the water, rice, and salt into a bowl. "Maybe he'll fall asleep." Max didn't like rice, she remembered with a grimace, unless it was smothered with impossibly hot curry sauce. The phone rang, but proudly efficient, she took the time to press all the proper buttons to set the microwave. The phone was on its third ring when she finally answered.

'Allô?'

'Oh, hi Daddy! It's me - Fanny.'

'Thanks. Yes, sixteen.'

'A poem? I didn't know you could write poetry.'

'Not even a cake. Mommy's gone to the clinic for the baby.'

'About ten o'clock this morning.'

'I don't know. I haven't heard anything. Hang on, I'll give you the number.'

She hunted for the address book, hoping he wouldn't ask to talk to the others. What would he think of her if nobody was home? Where were they, anyway? She'd heard the mo-ped, but Dad didn't want Max using it.

'I wish you were here, too. When are you coming back?'

'Oh, so long? I'll try. Bye-bye.'

Too bad he had called right then. He would worry. Except for her fright from Monsieur Griffon, everything *was* fine. The meal was on the way, the children were quiet, and even Nicky's burn wasn't bad. Her Dad's warm, happy voice gave her courage. Even Griffon's growls seemed less frightening.

Nicky's tape stopped and Fanny went in to turn it over. The room was empty. Nicky must have gone to Caroline's room. They were probably drawing together as usual. She turned the tape recorder off and pushed Max's book bag aside with her foot. As she answered the summoning buzz of the microwave, she slammed the front door shut impatiently. Max again. Today that door revived bad memories. It would be better closed and locked.

Nicky had indeed gone off to find Caroline, but she wasn't in her room, or in the bathroom. His finger hurt and he didn't like the bandaid. He pulled at it, but that hurt too. He looked downstairs in Mommy's room, but Caroline wasn't there either. He went back through the living room and out through the big front door. No one in the garage, or on the lawn; no one riding a bike. Nicky saw his big ball out in the field and ran to get it. It had a leak, and was soft. Instead of picking it up, he gave it a hard kick, and another, and another. Soon he was lost in weeds as high as his knees, but Nicky had only eyes for his ball, blue, red, and white. His Daddy had bought it for his birthday. He kicked and ran, kicked and ran. He forgot to look for Caroline.

Suddenly, right in front of him, was an enormous black dog. Nicky stopped, but the dog wanted to play with Nicky's ball, which it seized in its mouth, shook back and forth, and then dropped. Nicky ran to pick up the ball, but the dog grabbed it and ran away again. Nicky, laughing now, called out, '*Viens ici, gros chien! C'est mon ballon!*'

French was his outside language. Of course the dog would speak French. But the big black dog didn't seem to care that it was Nicky's ball.

Through the weeds and poppies they ran, the dog leading them ever closer to its home. Then, without warning, it dashed off behind a red van parked at the edge of the field and crawled under it, hiding from

Nicky. The little boy found himself staring up into the dark entrance of the back of the van.

Here was something even more exciting than a dog. Nicky remembered the ride in the yellow bull-dozer last summer when the men came to do the garden. Maybe he could sit on the driver's lap again in this truck. He began crawling up the wooden plank that stretched from the grass to the floor of the van. He was happy. It was easy. There were little ribs of wood nailed across. It was even easier than the slides at the playground. He stood up tall and stretched his arms out, walking straight up and in. But the black labrador had not forgotten Nicky, and dashed up behind him with the ball squashed between his sloppy jaws. He knocked Nicky over onto the dirty floor of the van and the two of them tumbled around playfully, both tugging at the ball.

* * *

Caroline was wakened by three things. First, the noise of a barking dog; second, a gurgling feeling of hunger; and third, a sore shoulder, where the edge of a stone had been pressing its way into her skin over the last half hour. She rubbed at her left arm, and stretched both hands in the air to get the kinks out. She looked down at her watch, knowing it must be late from the sudden coolness in the air and the angle of the sun at her back. Oh goodness! Five to seven already. Nearly time for supper. Where was her sketch pad, and why had she fallen asleep? Her only chance for bird-watching was gone now. She couldn't hope to do much tomorrow with Nicky at her heels all day. There was that dog again. She found her sketch pad and pencils among the dead oak leaves that had gathered at the foot of the crumbling wall. She patted at her pocket, remembering the camera. She'd better get back home. Fanny would be upset with her if she wasn't back on time.

Whose dog was that, having so much fun? She glanced out through the window of the hut in the direction of the joyous barking. There it was, a big dog, jumping in and out of that old red van at the edge of the field. It had a ball in its mouth and was playing with someone. The ball looked like Nicky's, but she had just seen it when she had come out of the house a short time ago. Was that the same dog that had come to the house last year?

She clambered out through the broken rubble of the hut and began the trek back home along the hillside. Suddenly Caroline stopped dead. Surely that was Nicky's happy voice she had just heard, mixed with the playful yelps of the dog. Nicky's voice, Nicky's ball... Nicky wasn't in the back of that truck! She had passed the van by on her left, but turned now and looked back down the valley. The van was blocked from view by the weeds. She pushed through the undergrowth to get a clearer view.

The dog was running up and down a sort of ramp leading into the back of the truck. And sure enough; this time Nicky's voice was distinct through the squeals of the dog. How had he gotten there? She would have to get him out, but the van was close to Monsieur Griffon's house and now that she might really have to, Caroline didn't want to meet that surly man! She suddenly remembered Fanny's warnings to stay away from the Griffon's property. Why had her sister been so insistent this afternoon?

She examined the house, the fields, the mass of broken cars to her left. No one was around, but she didn't call out to Nicky. Better to come up and call him softly. He would come straight to her. He had utter confidence in his 'Ca-wo-leen.'

* * *

At seven o'clock sharp Fanny rang the old Swiss cow-bell.

'Time to eat!' she called from the sliding door by the pool. There was no answering call from Caroline, no giggling, pell-mell run from Nicky, who loved his dinner. Fanny crossed to the heavy door where Monsieur Griffon had frightened her that morning. She opened it with dread, but met only a reddening sky. 'Nicky! Caroline! Max!' she called. 'Time to eat!'

The neighbour's cluttered field, empty of movement, lay waiting for the dark. Silence closed in on Fanny. She shivered and shut the door. Her mother's words rose in her memory to chide her, "Keep your eye on Nicky. He's only three." '*A table!*' she shouted desperately, as if French could work magic. But no one came.

6

ONLY ONE THING TO DO

Savagely Max turned the screw that held the hinge to the door of the fort. His mind dwelt on the woman he had seen in the distant kitchen, but he could do nothing. She was OK, he guessed. She had sat up after a while and bathed her forehead.

He should say nothing to the others about Monsieur Griffon. He mustn't scare them. He would tell dad when he got back from Germany. The screws were all in on an angle, but they held. Standing up, Max cocked his shoulders back, and dropped the screw driver into the side pocket of the mo-ped. The door worked pretty well. He could finish it some other time. It didn't matter anymore. He'd only finished it now to get his anger out. What sort of beast could treat people like that?

The sun was getting lower. Fanny would be serving supper at seven. He was hungry and had homework. It was probably close to seven now. His watch was broken; he and Jean-Francois had been fooling around and it had been smashed against a stone wall. He hadn't dared tell his parents since he had just lost a good jacket in February.

Thinking of the watch made him remember the binoculars for Caroline. He went back into the hideout and picked them off the ground where he had dropped them in disgust. Standing up, he noticed movement below and, against his own desire, he focused the binoculars on the blue tent. The same two men were emerging. They lifted up a flap of tarpaulin together, revealing a sleek, shiny black Peugeot with someone in the driver's seat. It moved slowly out of the 'garage' and toward the back of the large red van. Max could just hear the smooth purr of the engine. The black dog that had once found refuge at their house was cowering nearby chewing on a multi-coloured ball.

The two mechanics stood near to guide the driver up the makeshift ramps and into the back of the truck, but he didn't need it. He drove without hesitation straight up and into the van. Max lost his movements in the shadows, but saw him jump back down, slam shut the two back doors, and lock them with a padlock. It was Monsieur Griffon himself. He waved one of his workers impatiently out of the driver's seat, where the man had brought the heavy engine to life. Then he hoisted himself into the cab and guided the van slowly across the field to the driveway.

What set Max's heart thumping crazily were several facts, which took some time to register. Just before the doors had slammed shut, and almost like a shadowy vision, a flash of blue, a trace of blonde hair, and a form like that of Caroline's had appeared. As he froze inside at the possibility, so outlandish, that she might be in the back of that van, his eyes continued to wander through the binoculars for a few seconds. There was something on the ground near the back of the truck - a drawing pad. Then he remembered the ball. Quite like Nicky's. How had the dog come across the ball, if it was Nicky's? And what did that have to do with the truck, with Caroline, with her bird-hunt?

* * *

Caroline climbed in to get Nicky, who saw her coming and decided to hide in a tool box toward the front of the compartment. She set her sketch pad on the ground, clambered up the ramp with more difficulty than Nicky, and tried to pull him out of the long cupboard that walled off the cab from the back of the truck. But his foot was stuck, and it took some manoeuvering. Before she could manage it, she heard with horror the arrival of a car, which was coming straight at the van. She tried to hurry Nicky along, but this only made him cry harder, as his foot was twisted behind a box of tools so heavy that she had no chance of moving it.

The black Peugeot moved steadily up the ramp and into the van. "Quick," she told herself. "Crawl back into the hole with Nicky!" It was silly not to call out just then, but panic seized her, and she had to avoid the car's bumper. The driver got out of the car and jumped down. She thought better of her fear and decided to call for help. But her first shouts were muffled by the cupboard and then the truck's engine roared. She had to shout even to Nicky as she told him to hold still for a minute.

By the time she got to the doors, they were already clanging shut and her call for help turned into more of a squeak, easily masked by the grating of the hinges as the doors slammed closed. She heard the crunch of the lock with a shiver of dread. Her mind went into a daze. She had never dealt with a problem like this one. Nicky's frightened voice called her back into action.

'Cawoleen, *ou es-tu? J'ai peur!*'

'Don't be afraid, Nicky! I'm coming. Just hold very still.'

But Nicky couldn't hear her, and began screaming.

* * *

Max's thoughts chased faster and faster in his head and kept on chasing as he stuffed the binoculars back into the case, ran to his mo-ped and dropped them in the side pocket. He didn't really have time to think, but if there was the remotest possibility that Caroline or Nicky were in the back of that truck, imprisoned by Monsieur Griffon, whether accidentally or by design, there was only one thing to do. He jumped on the motor bike and pedalled as hard as he could. It often had trouble starting, but the rough road was downhill and the bike sputtered into action. Ten seconds later he was roaring down the dirt road, past the kitchen window, and up again on the south side of the valley, where their driveway joined the neighbour's at the top.

The red van was nowhere in sight. Probably it had already left. Which way had it turned at the pillars that marked the entrance to the two properties? The bike slowed noticeably as it struggled to conquer the steep drive. Never had Max felt so impatient with its sluggishness, but it crept up the worst of the slope and picked up speed gradually. There was the van, just disappearing around the bend. He had to catch it and tell Mr Griffon that his sister was stuck in the back. The man couldn't be so crazy as to harm him on the open road, could he? If the children weren't in the truck, then Griffon would think he was nuts, and so would Fanny, but so what?

7

BLACK

The van lurched forward and Caroline struggled to stay upright as they angled up the steep driveway. She could see nothing whatsoever except a few cracks of light in the walls of their prison.

'Nicky,' she called as she got closer. 'Have you got your foot out yet?' "Say anything," she told herself, "so that he can hear your voice."

'I'm stuck! I'm scared! It's dark!' So many fears. She shared them, but couldn't show it.

'OK! I'm nearly there. Where are you?' She groped along, using the smooth, warm surface of the car to guide her. She alone was responsible for Nicky now. He should be near the left headlight, she remembered. Leaning down, she pushed her hand into the blacker hole of the tool cupboard and discovered Nicky's leg. Twisting and struggling, she managed to get his right foot free, but his sneaker was swallowed by the black hole. She pulled her little brother to her, and they both pushed their way along the wall of the van to the back, where there was enough room to sit down. Caroline sat Nicky on her lap.

'I wanna go home. I'm hungry,' declared Nicky sullenly to the dark.

'I know, Nicky,' comforted Caroline. 'Me too. But I don't have anything here. We'll just have to wait until the truck stops to get out. I don't think anyone will hear us if we shout. There's too much noise.'

This logic meant nothing to Nicky. He kept on begging to eat, until Caroline got cross. This set him crying, and made Caroline feel bad. It was normal for a three year old to feel hungry at seven o'clock at night! She tried to snuggle his head onto her shoulder, but Nicky was angry by now, and tried to get away from her - to go where? Something had to be done.

She pulled Nicky gently down onto her lap. 'Now, Nicky,' she said firmly. 'The first thing we're going to do is pray.'

Caroline knew that Nicky always settled immediately when she prayed with him, which she did every night. As she spoke, she rocked him gently in the dark, soaking in the comfort of his warm body and the softness of his cheek against hers. Then, her voice barely breaking into sound, she half hummed, half sang Nicky's favourite lullaby. She felt his head go heavy as he relaxed. Caroline adjusted him carefully to relieve some of the pressure, and sat staring into the blackness. She tried to imagine herself lying in God's arms the way Nicky was in hers. Mommy always told them that God's arms were around them all through the darkest night. Somehow, though, the cold metal walls didn't feel much like arms. It was easier to imagine God at home under her warm quilt, but she needed Him more here. A lonely tear wandered down her cheek. She dared not rub it for fear of waking her little brother.

8

A TABLE LAID

Fanny poured water into four glasses and examined the table. Nothing missing. The chicken looked rather appetizing and since the others were late, she had even had time for a grated carrot salad with *vinaigrette*, which she made even better than Mom. Where were they all? She turned to the oven, pulled out the bowl and tasted a grain of rice. 'Stupid microwave,' she muttered. The rice was still hard. Max would never stop teasing her if she couldn't even get the rice right. "I'll have to cook it on the stove," she thought, transferring the rice from the bowl to a pan. As she set it on the flame, she saw Max roar by the kitchen window and on up the road on the moped. She dashed through the house, out the sliding door and onto the lawn. But Max was far up the driveway and the racket of the feeble engine died away as he disappeared out of the property.

'Now where's *he* off to at supper time?' said Fanny with a huff. And where were Nicky and Caroline?

Shrugging her shoulders in annoyance, she marched back into the house. On the coffee table her Agatha Christie mystery lay upside down and opened, inviting her to pick it up. Why not? After all, if they were all going to be so late, she might as well relax. 'You certainly deserve a break,' she told herself. She would just wait for the rice to cook.

But the words trotted along before her eyes, teasing, refusing to mean anything. When she had read and re-read three paragraphs, she lay the book down and stared out at the hillside, grey-green in the coming dusk. Fanny nibbled angrily at her nails. Where was Nicky right now? Should she go out looking? Mommy never seemed to worry about him. But her encounter with Griffon made things a little different. He was a crazy man.

Nicky wasn't in the pool. She had already hunted through the house, even checking the closets. He was nowhere within earshot. He would be with Caroline surely, wherever *she* was!

The phone jangled loudly and she jumped up, startled.

"Don't be so jumpy, stupid," she told herself. "This will be Caroline now."

'Allo?'

But it wasn't. An unknown woman's voice announced flatly that Thomas Ronald Castle had been born at 17:35. All was well. 2 kilos, 800 grams; a good weight for a premature baby. Mother was fine, but couldn't come to the phone. Was everything in order at home?

Fanny assured the nurse that all was well.

Hanging up the receiver, she lowered herself onto the rickety telephone stool. The hallway glowed red in the sun's setting rays. Everything was quiet.

This wasn't how it should happen. Where was Daddy, with an enormous bouquet of flowers hiding that secret smile of his? Why couldn't they all get in the car and ride over to the clinic like they had when Nicky was born? The nurses would scold and shoo, but let them in, all around the bed for a quick picture. She longed to hug her mother and pick up that moist, live bundle.

Instead, she remained at a distance, alone, trying to grasp a message from a cold-faced nun dressed in a starched, white gown. What did that nun know about babies? Why should she be the one to look after Thomas? Oh, the sisters were nice enough, she supposed, but it was she, Fanny, who was the real big sister! She frowned in jealousy, and sat staring at the white plaster wall. Her finger rubbed listlessly at the traces of the bird Nicky had drawn and tried to wash off.

Here she sat, alone and useless. She was supposed to be looking after the family and she didn't even know where they were! 'Oh, God, keep them safe,' she murmured, but the words felt slightly embarrassing. Was God even listening?

Suddenly an acrid smell burned into her mind, chasing images of white-faced nuns and downy baby heads. The rice! She looked at her watch as she dashed to the kitchen. 7:35! The rice was blackened hard onto the white enamel pan. Woodenly Fanny turned off the flame, and sank onto a kitchen chair. Laying her bewildered head on her solid arms, she sobbed.

9

MARSEILLE BY MO-PED

The van lumbered along winding country roads through fragrant pine forests near Max's home. He had nearly caught up with it. Scenes of car chases had flitted briefly through his mind, but this had nothing to do with that sort of adventure. He was simply following the truck to get his sister out of the back, and would have to wait until it stopped to get his message through to the driver. Cruel or kind, the man would at least look for the children.

At the same time he felt foolish, for the farther he went from home, the more ridiculous it seemed that his sister or brother was in that truck. It must have been his imagination. But, if they were? What else could he do but follow? The wind whipping through his hair drove his thoughts to flapping as uncontrollably as his sleeves. Go back to the Griffon's to find out where the truck was headed? Turn for home to see if Caroline and Nicky were calmly eating their supper right now? Speed up and pass the truck immediately? Flag the driver somehow. Max clung to this last idea lest it, too, be swept away by the wind.

But the truck slid into heavier traffic on a major road. Max had a stop sign, then several cars between him and the van. It was all the mo-ped could do to plug along behind them until they tired of the slow-moving van and passed it. As he drew near again, he noticed a police car hidden behind some trees beside the highway. He had no helmet! They would surely stop him.

The truck picked up speed. They were headed towards the freeway. How far would they go? What about gas? And mo-peds were illegal on the freeways. At least there were no tolls on this stretch. But what if they started going west, or swung back northwest to Lyon? He only had about three francs of odd change. If only he could sit still to think! All thought was overruled by the wind. By keeping his head tucked as far down as possible, he could barely keep his eyes open at these speeds. They constantly filled with tears, and he kept blinking hard and shaking his head to clear his vision. Threatening, bulbous street lamps hung over him. Microphones, he thought, reporting his movements to the police. Yellow eyes of some science fiction monster, watching, knowing.

Dismissing foolish imagination, he gave himself to one cause - following the van. It filled his mind and soul. He imagined himself tied to the padlock on those grey doors by an invisible rope. He had to follow. If he lost the van, no one would ever know where Nicky and Caroline had gone. What if Monsieur Griffon was a kidnapper as well as a car thief? If he could treat his own wife like that, what *would* he do to two little children? Nothing was unbelievable anymore. He was powerless now. But the van was still there. It was all that he could do, all that counted.

His hands and arms grew tired and numb from the constant vibration. His right hand, cocked at an awkward angle, held the accelerator at full speed. His whole arm ached. But the cold and his determination locked them into place and held them there. His short sleeves flapped wildly, stinging his upper arms. Looking at his speedometer, he was surprised to see that they were only going fifty kilometres an hour. It felt like a hundred and twenty. Were the police behind? Would they ever believe his story when they stopped him?

Stop him! How would he catch the van then? The licence plate. He had to remember the number. Memorize it now. He squinted, looking up. But the truck had gained distance on a hill. The number was hard to read in the dusk. Something FR13. The last number was easy. Thirteen for *Bouches-du-Rhône*. That was their *département*. "FR - like France," he thought. The rest... He could just see it now. 8765.

Suddenly Max was shoved violently off to the right as a gasoline truck barrelled past him. A horn blared and Max imagined the driver's angry gesture. He yanked on the handle bars, dragging them left, beginning to skid. The bike wobbled wildly and Max felt himself losing control. "This is it," he told himself. "I'm going to crash against the guard rail." He thought of his new sneakers. What a waste of money. He wouldn't need them. They'd be ruined. They didn't fit Nicky. Too big. How silly to think of such things. He saw lampposts, grass, cars. There were his own arms, stiff, thin. Useless now. He would never need arms again. But then, miraculously, he could see the dead red doors of the van, their tyres, the exhaust spluttering black. The bike steadied, and drew in line once again.

Max was now shaking from the fright of his near accident. It was too much. Unfair, this responsibility. He was alone, small. He wished himself gone, picked off his bike and dropped back onto the peaceful hillside. This would be a fine adventure for a book. But not for him, not here, not now. The van veered off gradually to the right and Max thought it might stop, but he noticed out of the corner of his eye the white exit sign *Vieux Port*.

Marseille sprawled around the old port, dangerous, enormous, overwhelming. Heavy rectangular apartment buildings stood row upon row, old and decrepit. Packed inhabitants waved distress signals on their laundry lines to passing motorists. The French held Marseille in smiling disdain, its citizens good only for standing in the breech against encroaching African immigrants. *Notre Dame de la Garde* lifted her eyes to heaven, afraid to face the problems of beleaguered Marseille as it slaved its way into dreary oblivion, important only to itself.

As the highway swung out on its high-flung loop over the water, Max tried not to look down at the monstrous pillars and the forlorn docks so far below. He had always hated Marseille.

10

WINE AND POTATO CHIPS

Caroline couldn't get comfortable. She sucked disconsolately at a scratch on her palm, which stung and throbbed. Nicky lay in peaceful abandon on her lap, his poor little knees on the dirty floor of the truck, his head trustingly tucked against her thigh. She shifted carefully, searching yet again for some position that didn't hurt. As she did, the truck lurched suddenly. Nicky's head banged the unforgiving metal of the doors, and he pulled himself up, moaning. '*Je dois faire pipi*,' he whined to Caroline. She could feel him fumbling at his belt.

'Oh no, not here, Nicky!' She struggled out of the cramped corner and herded Nicky by feel through the dark into the farthest corner of the van. Pipi was one thing. What would she do when he wanted to do something else? There were no bathrooms in this hotel! As Nicky finished, she had an idea for sleeping. There might be no bathrooms, but there was a bedroom - the car.

'Come over this way, Nicky. I have an idea,' she said as brightly as she could in the middle of that cold, miserable night.

'I think I can find a bed for you.'

'I wanna go home,' protested Nicky, as he shuffled along the side of the invisible car. 'I wanna see mommy.'

'I know, Nick. Me too,' sympathized Caroline. She had found the handle of the back door. Reaching around Nicky's shoulders, she tugged the door open and encouraged him into the back seat. But Nicky was not to be comforted.

'I'm cold!' he sobbed. 'I'm hungry!'

Caroline sighed and stripped off her sweat shirt. She was already cold with it on! Shivering in her thin tee-shirt, she struggled to get her sweat-shirt on Nicky in the dark. It felt inside out. Who cared? At least if Nicky were warm, he might go back to sleep. She lay down on the welcomingly soft car seat, and helped Nicky snuggle in beside her. Maybe she could still get a little warmth out of her sweat shirt. Nicky nuzzled gratefully into her embrace, flinging his warm little hand around her neck, and toying with her hair. He fell sound asleep.

Not so Caroline. She lay awake cold and fearful, listening to the unfamiliar rumbles around her. She hugged at Nicky as hard as she dared, but sleep defied her. The back seat, so welcome only moments ago, now began to threaten her. A rotten smell of stale wine and eggs filled the stuffy interior of the car. She shuddered uncontrollably. She couldn't possibly lie still for one more second. Even her legs tingled and twitched. They might be cooped up here forever! The truck would be parked in a vacant lot for six months and they would never get out! No one knew they were here. She and Nicky could even die. Images floated through her mind in the dark. Too horrible to speak, too horrible to dream. She could imagine Monsieur Griffon's leering face, grinning in triumph and excitement through the dark windows.

Caroline sat up hard and straight, gasping, and holding back a scream. She screwed her eyes tight, trying to black out the screen, but all she could see was fat lips curling over big yellow teeth, laughing. She wished herself back under her silky quilt. She forced herself to transform the hideous face into the face of her mother; the shining auburn hair, her soft, trusting eyes, narrowed by cheeks high with joy and affection. Caroline clung tightly to Nicky's feet as a drowning man would cling to a buoy.

"Be sensible!" she told herself. "Do something with your hands. Don't just sit conquered by imaginations! Monsieur Griffon is far away. There's nothing to worry about - you're just stuck in a car." She fumbled about with her hands in the dark, following the fuzzy seat ahead of her. Blind people could tell colours by feel. Maybe she could now, if she tried. She ran her hand down the back of the seat in front of her. The frame, hard metal. The floor, carpeting. A package, cloth. It was a zip bag. "Explore. Discover.

Bring yourself back." Caroline unzipped the bag. A woolly jacket. A picnic lunch.

A picnic lunch! She should eat. There was a bag of snack food. She *should* eat. It would do her good. She tugged at the sealed bag. The package broke open and the unmistakable odour of potato chips suddenly covered the disagreeable smells around her. She lay a chip on her tongue. The salty burst of flavour surprised and relieved her. She nearly laughed. This was real. This chased away the fear. How could a potato chip make her happy?

Out of the dark unknown the thought of communion came to her mind. It was the flat wafers she had seen at her friend's Catholic church. They reminded her of the potato chips. The words she had heard so often in her own church floated into her head: "This is my body broken for you." She kept munching. Then other words from the Bible. They seemed new to her tonight, as if God Himself were whispering them in her ear. They weren't from the communion service this time: "I will never leave you or forsake you." Caroline stopped chewing.

'Are you here, God?' she whispered, through the mush in her mouth. 'Here in this black truck?'

Silently the answer came.

"Where two or three are together in my name, I am there."

Two or three. Well, she was one, and Nicky made two. And they did have the right 'name'. Daddy always told them that their very first name was Christian, even before Caroline, or Nicky. God had adopted them into His family, so they all shared Christ's name. Hers was Christian Caroline Eloise Castle. Of course they didn't say the 'Christian' part out loud.

'In your name,' she said out loud, and put another potato chip in her mouth.

Caroline suddenly knew in the deepest depths of her inside self that she was not alone. Max wasn't here to help her, but she had a better big brother, a perfect one. Jesus *was* here, as He had promised. And if He could be so alive after dying, maybe death wasn't so real after all.

"There's something deeper than death," she thought. "Something more real than the dark." And there with Nicky trustingly asleep on her knees; there sitting in the black lap of fear, Caroline gave her body as well as her soul into God's care.

The potato chips made her thirsty. She reached into the bag blindly. Strange that she should find a bottle of wine. She certainly was thirsty. So what if it was wine? Fortunately it was half gone, otherwise she never could have opened it. As it was, she still struggled with the cork. It popped loudly, and Caroline laughed out loud. Wine for communion. She drank deeply, grateful for the drink, grateful for the blood of Jesus, poured out for her.

And so it was that in the back seat of a mysterious Peugeot, Caroline Castle took what she always considered to be her first communion. She never dared to tell anyone about it. She supposed they would not approve; communion was for church, and rightly so. She knew something happened that night. It was not just how real God was to her there in the dark. That was feelings, and who else would know? What surprised everyone, and not Caroline the least, was that she suddenly lost the need to 'borrow.' The day her official first communion took place, Caroline could only taste potato chips, and wore only her own jewellery.

Now, warmed by the wine and oddly carefree, she pulled the woolly garment from the bag, successfully inserted her arms into it in the dark, and snuggled back down beside Nicky. She stroked his hair with a gentle hand, wanting to share in some way the mystery she had discovered. Wine and fatigue soon carried her, as it had Nicky, into sleepy oblivion. As the red van pulled into the walled-in courtyard of *36, Allée du Lavoir*, Caroline and Nicky never realized that it had stopped.

11

THE TUNNEL
AT THE END OF LIGHT

Max remembered coming along this highway when they had taken the car-ferry to Corsica. But the enormous pillars and the dark, haunting waters below took on new proportions to him now. No longer did the solid walls of a car envelop him in a serene bubble, untouchable, and secure. He was fragile, miniature, vulnerable - and stiff with cold. The sun's rays cast bleak shadows as they tried in vain to penetrate the squat buildings at the dockside. Heavy vessels with ugly lines settled deep into sluggish waters as if to disappear in some final, sinking sleep, dragging all of Marseille, and Max himself along. He tried to speed up, to stay just ahead of those tentacles of fear that threatened to snag him, but ahead loomed only the sickly yellow lights of the harbour tunnel. The tunnel! He had forgotten there was a tunnel.

Max slowed suddenly and drastically, causing a blue Volvo behind him to veer dangerously to avoid him. He *couldn't* go into a tunnel. He just couldn't do it. The mo-ped pulled off to the shoulder and came to a standstill. Max watched the red van disappearing. He pounded his fist on the handlebars. Was there no other way around? He would go anywhere, do anything. But not a tunnel!

'Car-o-liiine! Niiiicky!' he screamed to the heavens, his head laid back. He bellowed out his tension, oblivious to the stares of passing motorists. The van was small, distant, in the tunnel. Gone, under tons of water.

All his nightmarish memories floated back. The dark, gaping man-hole, lid lifted, inviting. His friends jeering, coaxing, daring him. Sudden dank, foul smells. Then the shock of cold water, pouring over him, around him, overwhelming, choking him. He was floating, half-dead, lungs aching. No way out. Struggling, drowning. His head knocked on cement. Oblivion. They had thought him dead when they had dragged him out.

He had never entered a tunnel since. His dad found ways around them when they were driving. How had they gone to the ferry last summer? There had been no tunnel.

The van was gone. What would happen to little Nicky, to innocent Caroline? He remembered the flat-faced woman, the blows.

Max stuffed his tongue between his molars and bit down on it decisively. With a violent tug he twisted the accelerator to full power. The old mo-ped skipped and jerked onto the road, swerving wildly, picking up speed. Max bit down harder and harder. It hurt. His knees clamped together like a vice. His arms locked. He screwed his eyes tight. There was no wind, but he left only the tiniest slit. He didn't want to see. Closer and closer came the sick light. The air warmed. Rhythmic bars of light marked his passage. So slow. He could feel the trap closing behind him with a rush. There would be no exit. The water above would drip, seeping through. Soon there would be a crack, widening. The foul water would rush down from above, burying him. He would never surface. Tons of rock, a world of water. It was roaring now in his ears. He would go under. The bike would die, the water was lapping at the tyres, dragging it under.

A slap of cold hit his face. Water! But the cold was refreshing and smelled only of the seaside. He was through, the tunnel behind him. Shaking and sweating, his tongue aching, Max felt a surge of elation. He had done it! He had surfaced into the cool, beautiful dusk of the May evening and was driving along the road that stretched along the old port. A prickly forest of masts wound round the harbour. A few old fishing boats were still sputtering into berth and the last of the touring boats was just arriving from the *Chateau d'If.*

But Max was frantic anew. He cut across the lanes on an angle, looking for the truck. Scores of cars competed for the best lane. Where was the van? Could it have turned the other way along the coastal road? There! He could see it far ahead, turning up a side-street on the right. Long minutes passed before he reached the intersection. He turned right where the van had turned. His bike laboured up a steep hill away from the water and into a run-down neighbourhood smelling of fish and urine. The mo-ped struggled with the steep grade.

Then two things happened. Max saw the tail end of the van just disappearing into a tiny cross street on the left, and he felt his bike die under him - out of gas. He jumped off and yanked it disgustedly to the edge of the road. He couldn't leave it in the middle of the street. He would have to drag it with him and hope that the van had stopped in the alley ahead. If not, then the search was over, after all he had gone through. Bending forward against the hill, his head nearly lying on the battered old seat, he shoved the heavy bike up to the corner. There he stopped, panting heavily, to survey his surroundings. He was in a cul-de-sac. The narrow alley ended about a block away. This was encouraging, but the truck had disappeared. Slowly, undecidedly, Max pushed his bike along the sidewalk. His steps were heavy and slow, his body shaking with cold and fatigue. Behind him the sun had given up trying to brighten the dark waters of the Mediterranean.

12

A FITFUL REST

Fanny stood high on the north side of the valley, frantically scanning every bush. Tonight she remained unmoved by the fabulous blaze which the May sun left in its wake as it plunged below the line of pines down the valley. Beneath her lay Monsieur Griffon's dreary sprawl. She had made a dozen phone calls to friends. No one knew anything. She had run from the neighbours on the other side to the shepherd's hut, calling and shouting until she was hoarse. The worst possibility now loomed before her - Griffon.

Her mother's voice echoed in her mind. "Keep your eye on Nicky. He's only three. Keep your eye on Nicky. Keep your eye on Nicky." Max would have known what to do. He knew better than to go roaring off at supper time. Why wasn't *he* here to help? And where could Caroline and Nicky be? At least Griffon hadn't been interested in them. It was Max who was in trouble, and he was safe. But she wished she had warned Caroline in stronger terms. She hadn't wanted to frighten her. She tried to think when she had last seen Caroline. They had bandaged Nicky's finger together. Then what? She must have gone out on that silly bird-hunt, of course. Had Nicky followed her? If they had wandered onto the neighbour's property, he might be holding them, or calling the police. Fanny looked down on the rusty cars, the dishevelled garden, the broken-down sheds. She couldn't go over there. Griffon would shoot her.

As she picked her way gingerly down the steep path, she wondered how Max could possibly ride down here on his mo-ped at top speed. He would do anything, she thought with admiration. If only she could be like him. He wouldn't be moping around wondering what to do right now. He would act. He would go to the neighbour's and ask after the children. He didn't care what anyone thought of him. He wouldn't even be afraid of a shotgun. He was so courageous, so full of joy and abandon, whereas she, Fanny, was paralysed by public opinion, no matter what the public! She was useless. Good for nothing. No initiative.

Silly wasting time on such thoughts right now. She should be thinking of Nicky. Anything could happen to a three year old. Why just last December Nicky had fallen in the pool trying to 'fish.' It was Caroline who had jumped in to save him - in her Sunday dress in the middle of winter. And she'd pulled him out, what's more. Fanny had never done anything spectacular like that. Everything in her life was so ordinary.

The phone was ringing as she arrived at the front door. Swinging the door open heavily, she dreaded answering.

'Allô?' Madame Didier's warm, low voice struck her ear. Immediately she realized that she would have to tell her. Maybe the children would come bursting through the door at any moment, but maybe they wouldn't, maybe never. She couldn't pretend any longer. She needed help. '*Oui, maman va bien.*' She recounted what few details she knew about her baby brother's birth. Madame went on and on asking her about the baby. How heavy was he? Did he look like *maman* or *papa?* Did the birth go well? Were there any complications?...

But Madame Didier, though nearly illiterate, was an astute judge of people. She noticed Fanny's lack of enthusiasm.

'*Qu'est-ce que tu as, ma grande?*' she asked gently.

Fanny breathed in deeply. Madame Didier was the last person who could help; she never drove at night and her knee was not yet healed from the operation. It would be a sacrifice for her to come tomorrow. Fanny had no desire to upset her, but she swallowed her pride, for Nicky's sake.

'*A vrai dire,*' she began, and then told Madame Didier her worries. They came out in a flood. But she didn't mention Monsieur Griffon's visit. Her mind would not allow the worst. It was all she could do not to weep. She was alone in the house. It was nearly nine o'clock, and quite dark.

'They're just not anywhere, Mamie Simone! I've looked all over.' After opening her heart, Fanny almost regretted it. Madame Didier scolded her, though gently, for letting Nicky out of sight. And instead of calming her, the older woman panicked, suggesting ugly possibilities, each more horrible than the last. Had she checked the pool? Poisonous products in the garage? The bathtub? The road up above? Had there been any strangers at the house? Many children were kidnapped these days. Kidnapped...kidnapped...

Fanny imagined Monsieur Griffon shaking Nicky, knocking Caroline around...tying them up in a dark closet.

'Madame Didier, what do you think I should *do*?' she asked desperately.

There was a silence, and then... 'You'll just have to call the police, *peuchère*,' admitted her French *mamie* with a sigh. She would come over at first light tomorrow morning. Was she sure she would be all right in the night? Fanny should call if they got home, even in the middle of the night.

She hung up, and looked for the number of the *gendarmerie*. She lifted the receiver, then put it back and sat down to compose her story. She would sound so irresponsible! She dialled, her heart thumping. Clearing her throat, she recounted her story to a disembodied voice. It sounded thoroughly ridiculous. Her sister and brothers were late for dinner! She probably wasn't hysterical enough to be taken seriously. Finally he said, '*Un instant*,' and passed her to a kindly man with lots of questions. Fact by fact she shifted her worries to the benevolent policeman. Here was someone strong, who could do something. Her spirit lightened, but quickly sank again. No search would begin until the following morning. Officers on duty in the area would be alerted. Did she want them to alert the clinic? No, no, by all means, no. (What good could it do to have her poor mother lying in a panic too? She couldn't do anything from her hospital bed! "What a stupid idea," thought Fanny.) Did she want a policeman posted to watch the house? 'No, thank you,' she replied. What for? To stop the children from coming home? To stop her from getting out? These were useless ideas. She needed someone to help her *look*, to *trace* them, to *find* them. She'd heard of people hunting all night for lost children by flashlight. Why did they have to wait nearly twelve hours before hunting for her family? Just to make sure the children would *really* be in trouble!

Her neck throbbed in anger.

She should call again tomorrow after eight if the children had not shown up, instructed the voice. Fanny slammed down the receiver. A heavy cloud settled over her heart. Her mother was in a nearby clinic blissfully enjoying her new brother while she, Fanny, had probably killed little Nicky. She threw herself down on the couch. Her mind was dead and tears remained in some play world, reserved for those who had problems with boyfriends. She lay utterly silent until a deep moan escaped.

Why had God chosen to punish her? Where were all

those guardian angels caring for and protecting them, especially dear Nicky whom she loved so? If the angels were only a nice idea, what about God Himself? He was powerful enough to avoid things like this. Either He wasn't powerful, or He didn't care. Didn't He realize she was only doing her best?

Her best? She had been trying to prove to Max how great she was. Maybe God was punishing her for being over-confident. But did that merit spiteful retribution? Did God get back at people? What sort of God was He, anyway?

Fanny lay in silent anguish. Occasionally, she dropped into fitful sleep. Twice she wandered around the entire house, turning on every light, convincing herself that she was alone. Maybe Max at least had sneaked back in. She turned each light off methodically after her. She peered out into the pitch black of the countryside. All was utterly still, utterly empty.

Wakened once again, this time by the cold at 3 a.m. she stumbled to her room and crawled under her covers. A bright moon poured its rays through her window, catching the plaque on her wall. "I will lie down and sleep in peace, for you alone, O Lord, make me dwell in safety."

'Huh,' snorted Fanny to herself. She turned over and faced the wall. 'Prove it, then.' She knew King David had known real fear, real loneliness when he wrote those lines from Psalm 4. Maybe he wrote that verse when King Saul was stalking him to kill him. But how could he say that? How could anybody "lie down in peace and sleep" if he knew someone might chop his head off in the middle of the night? It didn't make sense. It was completely ridiculous. Was she supposed to pretend that everything was wonderful? Just lay her sweet little head on the pillow and go off to sleep, nightie-night, Fanny? Nicky was dead somewhere in the lonely woods, and she was to lay her head down and sleep in peace? The dull ache of guilt and loneliness throbbed in her soul, overwhelming, as a flood of tears washed over her. Finally, she slept a little.

13

36, ALLÉE DU LAVOIR

Max plodded slowly along *l'Allée du Lavoir*. The truck had definitely turned down this lane, but had vanished. It must have pulled into a courtyard or garage. What had seemed so simple in his own neighbourhood - catching up with the truck to see if his sister was trapped inside - now seemed an enormously complex and dangerous operation. At dusk in a deserted alley at the Marseille dockside, anything could happen. Drug lords were regularly gunned down in Marseille bars. Car theft was rampant, illegal immigrants could be desperate. He, Max, fourteen years old, was not equipped to handle 'anything.' His family had always teased him when he had proposed various ideas about the dead Peugeots and the gangster-like visitors to Monsieur Griffon's house. He wished Fanny would dare to laugh now! His theories were pale next to the reality of what he was now living. Even he had not really believed them then. He did now.

He glanced around him, trying to notice anyone suspicious. Walking his mo-ped slowly along the narrow, filthy sidewalk, he tried to look purposeful and innocent. Just a boy who lived on this street coming home for the night. He was getting close to the end of the cul-de-sac and thought that if anyone was watching, he would not look so purposeful on his way *back* along the other side. He noticed a gate slightly ajar, though chained. Through the crack he could see the red van. Without stopping, he passed the gate and stooped to chain his mo-ped to a green lamppost. As he turned the key in the lock, he heard a side door swing quietly open. He wanted to run, anywhere. His heart was beating crazily, but he forced himself to keep his head down, concentrating on the lock, hoping whoever it was would pass him by unnoticed.

Out of the corner of his eye he could see a stocky, dark man, crossing the street, lifting his shoulders and rolling his head this way and that, as if it were stiff. When the man was halfway across the road, a whining sound came from behind him. Without thinking, Max looked back curiously. A large black dog bounded out of the same door and came slinking behind the dark figure in the road. As Max's eyes followed the dog, recognition flooded over him. He knew the dog. He knew the man. It was Monsieur Griffon himself and he was nearly within reach! Max turned his head quickly back to his mo-ped, but not before Monsieur Griffon's glare had taken him in. The stocky man stopped. Max forced himself to lean over his mo-ped, as if checking the air in his tyres.

Would Griffon remember the day at Max's house? Or was he one of those adults who never noticed children anyway? For once Max would be glad if he were. The dog, too, had noticed Max. For an instant his head had come up and his tail had set to wagging. Max sensed the man watching him. Then Griffon cowed the dog with a foul word and an angry kick, and moved across the road.

'*Pas possible...*', Max heard him mutter. He looked up in time to see him enter 36.

"Now, what?" thought Max to himself. He sat down on the dirty sidewalk, partially hidden from the view of anyone in 36. He remembered his screwdriver and binoculars and slipped them out of the mo-ped sidebag. He didn't want to sit here where he could be seen. He would find out if Caroline was in the truck.

The gate into the house was easy to climb, though the strap on the binoculars got tangled over one of the spikes at the top. Max dropped quietly into the courtyard. The van was there, sure enough. He had looked at that licence plate long enough to recognize it! He walked all around the van, knocking and calling as loudly as he dared.

'Caroline! Nicky! Caroline! Are you in there? Answer me.' His tinny knocks went unanswered, as did his whispered calls. There was no sound at all from the interior of the truck. Max argued once again with himself, remembering the notebook, the glimpse of blond hair, the ball. They *must* be in there. And if they were, they would be scared silly.

Still, there was little he could do to verify it. He couldn't knock on a neighbour's door in what was hardly a *quartier residentiel*, and ask people he didn't know to break into a truck that wasn't theirs on the basis of some stupid kid's wild stories about his sister and brother! Pulling out the screwdriver, he fumbled in the twilight trying to force the screws at the back around the padlock. But it was hopeless. He couldn't see well enough, and they were rusted anyway. He was afraid of being arrested for breaking into someone's property. Monsieur Griffon could easily drag *him* to the police, which would accomplish nothing for Caroline and Nicky.

He retired into a corner for some hard thinking. Maybe he was blowing all this way out of proportion. OK, Monsieur Griffon knocked his wife around. But he might have perfectly legitimate business in Marseille. He was simply letting himself be frightened by the oncoming darkness, by unfamiliar surroundings, by his loneliness.

His head buried between his knees, fingers running again and again through his hair, Max struggled to find some reasonable solution. But unless Caroline and Nicky were to spend the whole night in the dark van, there was nothing else to do but that which he most feared.

He stood up and sucked in a long breath, shuddering and rubbing his stiff right arm with his left hand, as if to remind himself of what he had already been through.

Then he stretched tall and walked deliberately over to the gate. It was not so easy to climb from the inside. The street was deserted. Distant traffic noises and the heavy Marseille accents of men arguing and joking in a nearby bar floated off to sea with the gulls. All seemed part of a world far away and out of reach. No one knew. No one cared. He stood in the lamplight at 36 before a darkish green door, chipped and peeling. The old stone steps were uneven and slippery with wear. He could barely make out a name on the faded bronze plate. Max reached up and punched the bell before he could change his mind.

After two rings he heard shuffling steps and the sound of someone working at the latch. The door swung inward revealing a reddish-haired woman whose age was impossible to determine. She was dressed in a sleazy, brightly flowered dressing-gown and smelled of wine. She grumbled something incomprehensible at Max. He couldn't tell if she was speaking Arabic or heavily accented French. She hung out the door over Max, who could not step back for fear of losing his footing. Her yellow teeth had smudges of bright pink lipstick and her skin was a sickly orange.

'*Excusez-moi, madame,*' squeaked Max, aware of the aggressive question in the woman's green eyes as his silence became embarrassing. 'I'm looking for the driver of that truck over there.' His right forefinger motioned half-heartedly toward the alley behind him. But the woman only stared at him, then turned abruptly on her embroidered sandal and bumped the heavy door shut with her oversized rump.

Max wrinkled his nose and stuck out his tongue. He drew it back in immediately, however. 'Oh, darn! That hurts!' he muttered to himself, kicking an empty package of Gaulloises cigarettes off the sidewalk and into the gutter. The gate again, then, he thought.

'*Connais pas*,' was all he had understood from the woman's drunken speech. He doubted that, since he had seen Monsieur Griffon go into that apartment with his own eyes. Back to his original plan, if it could be called a plan. Stick with the van. For the third time that evening he hitched himself over the pointed bars of the gate and dropped into the sandy courtyard.

Looking around, he discovered in the gloom a metal fire-escape stairway that curled around the corner of the courtyard. He could sit in the little nook about two stories up. He clambered up and settled onto the black metal landing. It turned out to be a good enough spot. He was not likely to be noticed from below. Protected from the sea breezes here in the corner of the sheltered courtyard, he was not uncomfortable, though extremely hungry.

From this height he could just see out over the roof of the house opposite, and down to the harbour. With his binoculars he surveyed the cluster of yachts. At one section of the harbour, he could see all the way to the other side, and made out a nun riding by on a bicycle with four large loaves of bread, the ones they called *restaurants* strapped to her back. It made him think of Maria in the 'Sound of Music,' and he wondered if the sister was late from spending too long wandering and singing in the *callanques*, those rocky hills near the coast? Or did the sisters have to eat that bread tomorrow morning, already stale from a few hours in the air? *Bread!* It was enticing enough to tempt him away from his goal. Could he go and get something to eat? Could he risk leaving the courtyard? What if the truck left in the meantime? The gate was locked for the night, probably. It seemed unlikely that the van would drive out soon. He dug in his pocket and tried to count his change in the shreds of light forgotten by the parting day. There were at least two one-franc pieces, one fifty-centime piece, a few tens and twenties. Enough for a three franc loaf of bread, he concluded.

He tucked the money back into his pocket and lay his head back against the crumbling stone wall built how long ago, by whom? How peculiar that he, Max, was sitting here right now. His mother in the clinic knew nothing of his whereabouts. His father, in Frankfurt probably didn't even know that the baby was on its way. Dad would be kicking his feet up in a hotel room to watch the news after a long day of meetings. He would have a cup of coffee and some German chocolate, or Swiss - even better. Max deliberately stopped thinking about chocolate. It was torture.

Nicky and Caroline, if they were in the truck, must be asleep. And poor Fanny at home, worried sick. Maybe instead of a loaf of bread, he should use the money on a phone call. But he just sat still, immobilized by the possibility of the truck escaping from view. Without knowing why, he had made his decision yet again; stick with the truck.

He curled around the metal post that supported the bannister, and crooked his elbow onto the first step, laying his head along his arm. Max, too, finally dozed, though his companion was the night cold and his bed was iron.

14

PLENTY OF SOUP FOR TWO

Fanny woke early Wednesday morning. For the flit of a second, she thought she was facing a brand new day. Then reality smothered her. Nicky was dead, and she was a murderer. The silence was oppressive. She was still alive. She could think and feel. Too bad. She sat up in bed, and gazed out at the mist. She could see nothing of the valley or the trees around the house. Thick steam rose from the pool. She was utterly alone. She wasn't supposed to think she was alone. But God would just have to forgive her for wanting someone with skin on. Anyway, she'd have to forget God, now. After what she'd thought about Him last night, He wouldn't want to forgive her for anything. It was over between Him and her.

If only Nicky would come down and cuddle under her covers. If only Max would come begging for tea this morning. Early morning was a secret time, full of hope and newness and expectations. This morning the canvas was black, the music discordant. Nothing was as it should be. She longed to hear her father's hearty call, 'Where's that tea, Fanny?' as he burst out of the bedroom, freshly showered and shaved; or her mother's sweet, 'Good morning, darling. Did you sleep well?' Even Caroline's hopeless morning grunts would have been welcome.

She pulled on her bathrobe and wandered into the kitchen, her feet cold on the glazed tiles. Like a slap in the face, yesterday's withered remains shocked and humiliated her. The chicken lay cold on the table and the ruined rice taunted her. She forced herself to pass the table and move to the electric kettle. She needed a strong cup of coffee. She couldn't bear to drink tea alone, without the others. The motions of coffee-making settled her mind and she sat down in the living room to drink. The coffee burned. 'Go ahead. Burn me up. Not just my throat. All of me.' But she didn't burn. She sat in a chair.

Her gaze settled on the hillside which could just be seen through the lifting mist. The family Bible lay on the table. This is where she was supposed to find help. But she didn't want to open it. Only judgment awaited her there. But her mother's favourite verse sprang to mind in spite of herself. 'All things work together for good to those who love God.'

Even the forest fire which had killed her friend's father? Madame Didier's husband dying? Marie-Paule's excruciatingly painful cancer? The children getting lost? It just wasn't *true*. Things didn't always work out for the best. Her brain wearied of trying to sort it all out. She wished she could curl up like a tiny little girl against her father's chest and not worry about anything anymore.

But Daddy wasn't there, and she was. She put her cup into the dishwasher and cleared off the table. The chicken went into the fridge. It was too early to call anyone, even the police. Mamie Simone should come soon. A shower did nothing. She felt just as dirty when she finished.

At eight o'clock she called the *gendarmerie* again. No news, but they would be sending a couple of men out to the house. Could she tell them how to get there?

Next she called Madame Didier, who was planning to leave soon and would stop to get something for lunch. Fanny didn't mention the chicken and somehow Madame Didier had it in her mind that they would all be together for lunch. She didn't dare say that there was probably plenty in the house for two.

Her mother called, full of the story of Thomas' birth. Happy, fulfilled, and complete. The baby was in her arms nursing as she spoke on the phone. When, as an after-thought, she asked Fanny if everything was fine at home, Fanny heard herself lie, 'Yes, Mommy. We're OK.' The doorbell rang and she hung up saying, 'Here's Madame Didier now. Bye-bye.'

But it was the *gendarmes*, businesslike, though one must only have been a few years older than she was. They took a few notes and left to search the neighbourhood. Madame Didier arrived in the meantime. Her big bear hug released Fanny's tears and

73

she sobbed for a long time before her adopted 'grandma' said, *Allez, viens. On va faire de la soupe, toi et moi*. And so with a dead heart, Fanny helped make soup at 9:00 a.m. for a family that wasn't there.

15

EARLY BIRDS

Max and Nicky woke at about the same time, though each was unaware of the other. Max felt only his gnawing hunger and decided that he ought to risk a loaf of bread. There was no movement in the courtyard and he noticed the door going out onto the sidewalk, probably the one Monsieur Griffon had used last night. Maybe it was open. He stretched carefully so as not to make noise, climbed down the staircase, and crossed the yard. The door was not locked and he swung it inward, slipping out into the colder air of the street. His bike was still locked to the lamp-post just to the right. He turned left and went back towards the busier roads. He knew where he was in Marseille. They had driven past here on their way to the American consulate. He was not wrong in assuming that even at this early hour with the sun just peeking over the crest of the hills behind the *corniche* that he would find the warm fragrance of a bakery. Indeed, he only walked for two blocks before he found one, and made quick business of buying a loaf.

His purchase left him with thirty-five centimes. Hardly worth putting in Nicky's piggy bank. As he retraced his steps to the strange courtyard, he munched on the crisp edges of a steaming piece of bread he had broken off. Whatever could he do next? He would have to confront the door again, get past the lady to Griffon himself.

* * *

Nicky had no idea where he was when he woke up. He didn't know what the loud grating sound was that had wakened him and let in the bright sunlight. It was exciting to wake up in a car. Maybe they were going on vacation. He mustn't wake Caroline - she was mean in the morning.

He climbed into the front seat and played with the steering wheel and the gear shift and pushed all the buttons. He got the windscreen wipers to work, and the indicator. He couldn't get the seatbelt fastened. Then he went on the other side and opened the glove compartment. There were some papers and a pencil. He took the pencil and drew a big lady on one, a man on another, until there was a nice picture on every page. At the bottom he made a big N for Nicky. He folded each paper neatly when it was done and put it in his pocket. He would show Mommy when she got home from the clinic.

He climbed into the back. He rolled down the

windows. Then he saw a bag with a sandwich in it. He munched happily on this until he got tired of chewing. He put the sandwich in his pocket and wiped his fingers on Caroline's sweat shirt. There was her camera. He picked it up and put the string around his neck as he had always seen her do. Then he needed to do a *pipi*. He climbed out of the back of the car into the truck. It wasn't dark anymore. He could see out the back. The truck was parked. He couldn't jump down, it was too high. He did a *pipi* out of the back of the truck. It was fun. Then he saw some pigeons. Maybe they were hungry. He pulled the sandwich out and began to throw little pieces out the back of the truck. They loved it and came right near.

Caroline wanted pictures of birds. He would take a picture of the pigeons. He put the camera up to his eye. He could see the pigeons in the little window. As he pushed the button, he could see two men in the little window. He took the camera away to look. Where did the men come from? Then he saw they had come through the little door behind the pigeons. They weren't nice men. Nicky went back around the side of the car and crouched down so the mean men couldn't see him. The men were shouting at each other. They used lots of bad words, like the kids at school sometimes. They talked about some papers and the car and then they opened the big gates to the courtyard. They drove a big black truck in, like the red one, but larger.

One man went away and the other one got in the black truck. Nicky sat down on the edge of the truck floor and watched the pigeons, swinging his feet.

There was Max! He had some bread.

'Max! Max!' Nicky's thin little voice echoed in the courtyard. *Je veux du pain*! But Max wasn't happy. He put his finger to his mouth and made an angry face. He didn't want to talk to Nicky. He wouldn't come through the gate. He went away and hid. Nicky couldn't jump down. He began to cry.

* * *

Max had been caught by surprise, not expecting Nicky, the man, the open doors. He pulled back into the shadow behind the wall. Nicky's lonely little form sat in the open doors of the red van. Tears trickled down his grubby cheeks. Max longed to dash in and grab him away from any danger, but something held him back. Would Nicky be better treated on his own? He was so little and inoffensive. The stocky back of Monsieur Griffon came into view from the other side of the courtyard.

'*Espèce de crétin!*' He yanked Nicky down off the van by one arm, spilling him onto the hard, dusty ground. Without looking back, he leaped into the truck with surprising agility and lowered himself into the driver's seat of the car. Max took advantage of these few seconds to dash into the gateway, scoop Nicky off the earth, and drag him much more roughly than he would have liked to the safety of a nearby alley. A mangy cat yelped as Max stood on its tail.

'Be quiet, Nicky!' whispered Max intensely. 'Where's Caroline? Is she in there, in the car?' Still sniffing, Nicky nodded. Max slid back out of his hiding place, Nicky hanging on his legs. No amount of frantic gesturing would make him stay in the alley. Keeping close to the wall, he positioned himself behind some garbage cans where he could see the van. The car slid down the ramps backwards, and turned in the wide space of the courtyard to point its nose toward the wide open gates. As the car turned, Max caught sight of Monsieur Griffon. He stepped back quickly to avoid being seen. He had had time only to glimpse the deep, angry scowl that was forever engraved on his neighbour's repugnant face.

The sleek car's engine purred smoothly in the silence of the early city morning. Max could just see Monsieur Griffon's movements through the crack of the heavy gate. The man's heavy form swung from watching back over his shoulder to a head-on position. He reached for the gears.

'LIONEL!' The raucous voice blared from a window across the street. Max could see a fat hand clutching the rotting wood of the shutter. He recognized the voice of the wine-soaked woman of last night. '*Téléphone!*' she bellowed. '*Vite. C'est Kaffi!*' The name had an electrifying effect on Monsieur Griffon. His jowls dropped even lower and his mouth pulled into a hard line. Without a word, he flung open the door of the car, leaving the motor idling, and stalked out the gate. Max lowered himself silently as far as he could behind the trash cans that blocked the sidewalk. For the second time in twelve hours Monsieur Griffon passed by close enough to touch.

16

ESCAPE

Max waited until Griffon's thick form passed into the hallway of 36. Carefully, cautiously, he poked his head around the corner of the gate. Through the front window of the car he could just see the wide eyes of Caroline peering over the edge of the seat. Then he made a decision more quickly, (and, he thought afterwards, more stupidly) than he ever had before. Grabbing poor Nicky up once again, he dashed for the black Peugeot. Without a word of greeting or explanation, he deposited Nicky through the open window into the back seat, half on top of Caroline. He slid in behind the driver's wheel and yanked the door shut. His Dad's car was quite similar, but he had only driven it around the back roads and up his driveway at home. He put the car into first gear, let off the hand brake and let it slide noiselessly out into the empty street. The right wheel went over the curb with a bump as Max tried to turn the car left.

'What are you *doing*, Max?' whispered Caroline in

amazement, pushing Nicky off her neck. 'You can't drive!'

But Max didn't answer. The engine revved high as he tried to use the unfamiliar clutch pedal. Before he could think of shifting gears, the car came to the corner.

'*Va-t-en, méchant!*' shouted Nicky suddenly, his head peering out the back window.

'Who's mean, Nicky?' asked Caroline

'Giffon! Giffon!' Nicky hid his eyes in Caroline's lap and put his hands over his ears.

'Max! He can see you. He's back there!'

But the black Peugeot had already turned down Duvalier and was heading towards the docks, still screaming in first gear.

Just as the car came to a stop sign, several things happened at once. A great black bulk came shoving through the open window, knocking Nicky and Caroline over. Max turned his head to see, and the car veered off to the right, stalling and crunching its way onto the curb, stopped dead by a post. All the children began shouting at once.

'Come on! Get out of the car!' yelled Max. Hurry up! Griffon's not far behind. Get out! Get out!

Caroline, more bewildered than afraid, was struggling to get the great black labrador off Nicky. 'Get off him! Get off! Do you hear? Come on! He can't breathe!'

Nicky, however, undaunted by the strange night he had just spent in the back of a truck, only remembered the wonderful tussle he had had with his great, warm friend the day before.

'*Arrête!*' he giggled, as the dog's rough red tongue lapped at his cheek and snuffled at the remains of the sandwich in his pocket.

Max was not to be stopped. No sooner did the car jolt into the pole than he jumped out of the front seat, and dragged at the dog, Caroline and Nicky. They didn't realize. They hadn't seen. They must not get into the hands of Monsieur Griffon! He was leaning into the car and had Caroline halfway out, when he felt an iron grip on his right shoulder. Suddenly he was spun backwards and jammed against the open car door. Stubby fingers twisted the leather strap of the binoculars, which still hung ridiculously around his neck, choking him, and pressing his head backwards over the door.

Caroline's eyes went wide and her heart thumped. Without a second's hesitation she did what she could. Swinging both legs up from the seat she kicked as hard as possible from her cramped position. They were aimless kicks, but they served well.

'*Sale gamine!*' bellowed Monsieur Griffon, and let go of Max long enough to finish dragging Caroline out of the car and dump her in the wet gutter. But Monsieur Griffon hadn't taken Nicky into account. Seeing his lovely Caroline treated like that got him boiling mad. This was not like wrestling with Max. The rules were different, and Nicky knew it. The handle of a screwdriver was sticking out of Max's pocket. He grabbed it and as Monsieur Griffon's rump came into full view and easy reach, he leaned forward and jabbed at it as hard as he could.

The results were spectacular. Monsieur Griffon exploded into a tornado of foul language and violent blows. They rained on Caroline and Max, who protected themselves as best they could. Nicky, still inside the car, was more fortunate. One more jab on his neighbour's leg, however, brought Monsieur Griffon's full fury on the little boy. Seizing Nicky by the hair and by one arm he dragged him out of the car. It proved to be his biggest mistake.

The black dog had been cowering on the floor of the Peugeot from the moment he had heard his master's voice. But when those stubby hands reached for Nicky, its head came up, and a reddish light smoldered in its sad eyes. How it could spring from such a cramped position remains a mystery, but spring it did. Its great jaws clamped onto Monsieur Griffon's right forearm just as the man was about to strike Nicky. Mr. Griffon fell back, but wrenched the dog's left paw out and away from its body. They all heard a sickening crack. The dog moaned in pain, but refused to open its jaws. There it hung, suffering, but dragging its disowned master to the ground. Max lost no time in scooping up Nicky in one arm, and dragging Caroline by the other.

'Let's go!' he shouted, and gave them no chance to protest. Caroline looked back over her shoulder to see the dog and Monsieur Griffon still rolling in the street.

The dog was just holding his own against Griffon's burly power. She tripped over a curb and Max pulled at her arm.

'I.. can't run... so fast,' she panted. But she could. She knew she had to. Her own camera was swinging wildly from Nicky's neck and kept bumping her in the face. The knit jacket she had put on in the car was far too big, making running a real chore. Max was as stiff as she was from the long night in the cold. It was just as well that the strap on the binoculars had snapped. He might have thrown them off anyway for speed. Caroline's eye felt sore and swollen, where Monsieur Griffon had knocked her against the curb.

They had started running along the main road by the harbour and Max pulled them through a few early morning shoppers in the fish market. They were a strange sight. Caroline could tell by the many stares.

'*C'est honteux!*' declared one elderly lady serving mussels behind a stall. 'Parents will let their children do anything these days!' Caroline supposed they did look shameful.

Max would not let them stop until they had gone all the way round to the end of the port and turned up a small road past the main avenue, *La Canebiere*. They sat down on the steps of a boarded up apartment in a narrow alley to take stock.

'Is he still after us, do you think?' asked Caroline, recovering her breath somewhat.

'I've no idea,' replied her older brother. 'But I don't want to hang around here! Where's Nicky's shoe? I can't carry him all the way to the station.'

'We lost it a long time ago in the truck. Why are we going to the station? How did you get here? And where did the dog come from? How did Monsieur Griffon get down here?'

'No time, Caroline. We'll have to sort all that out when we get home.' *If* we get home, he thought to himself.

'You wanna go home on the train, you mean?'

'I'm hungry!' moaned Nicky. 'I'm thirsty!'

But the lovely fresh bread was long since lost.

'We'll get you something as soon as we can,' promised Caroline. 'So how do we get home, then?' she reminded Max.

'Well, we lost the car,' teased Max. 'We can't walk all the way back home, and Fanny can't come for us. The train's the only thing left.'

'But I don't have my card, or any money either. What about you?'

'No card, and a grand total of thirty-five centimes.'

'What will we do?'

'Just let me worry about that. We have to get going. Come on.'

17

THE WEARY WAY HOME

The hard work of walking to the train station left them no energy for further discussion. They took it in turns carrying Nicky. Finally, after what seemed hours, they were forcing their tired legs up the grandiose flight of steps leading to the station. As they reached the top, Caroline, whose turn it had been to carry Nicky up the last ten steps, set him down. Shoe or no shoe, he could walk across the pavement himself. But for the second time that day a black form surprised them. This time, however, it was pitiful. The powerful dog could just barely drag himself along beside Nicky. His head was cut and bleeding. One paw hung useless as he hitched himself forward crookedly. Caroline wanted to stop and care for him, but Max wouldn't allow it.

Max was not happy to see the labrador. He stared back down the flight of steps, searching for a familiar, unwanted form. There were more people in the street now, and the train station was busy. Monsieur Griffon could be coming from any direction.

'Come on, let's find the train.' Where the dog is, *he* might be. Max led the way, Nicky followed with his hand over the dog's back.

They wound their way past bored travellers and a cleaning lady with her wide push broom. Nicky needed the bathroom, and the dog insisted on following. Even this early, tucked away in a remote corner of the restroom, there was no escaping the constant 'bing-bong' of the loudspeaker, announcing the arrival of some night train from Germany or the departure of the fast train to Paris. While she was washing Nicky's hands, and the dog watched patiently, a group of teenage girls burst in, giggling about their exciting adventures, bubbling over with stories of the boys they had met on their trip. She had a go at washing the dog's wounds with a paper towel, but they needed more, she could see.

Their travels today were not happy holiday times. Her tummy was in a knot and she wanted to get back to Max. When they returned to the bench where they had left him, he was gone! Her uneasiness gave way to panic. Max! Monsieur Griffon had come and taken him away. She looked around her wildly, but saw Max immediately, approaching on the run.

'Quick, Caroline. There's a train leaving for Aix in a couple of minutes. Let's go.'

'But what happens if the *contrôleur* stops us?'

'They never check tickets between Marseille and Gardanne,' replied Max with more confidence than he felt.

'They did when Daddy and I were on it last time. Anyway, it's cheating. Mommy and Daddy wouldn't want you to.'

'Well, it just can't be helped, Caroline. I've got no money and you've got no money, and we have to get home, don't we?'

Caroline, carrying Nicky again somehow, was puffing to keep up, and gave up the argument. If they got caught, she would just have to help Max explain what had happened. After what she'd just been through, it *didn't* seem very important about the tickets. She was glad Max was deciding everything. She could never have found even the train station, let alone the right train to take home.

As they rounded the corner to the train for Aix, a great crowd of German youngsters pushed by them. One with close-cropped hair and a gold sparkle pinned through his tiny ear nearly knocked her over. Nicky spilled out of her arms onto the filthy pavement. The boy mumbled what was probably an apology, but was too intent on catching his next train to help them up. Caroline felt suddenly tired and worn out. She began to cry quietly. Max took Nicky and carried him into the drab train car. The brown plastic seats had never looked so inviting. They were in the smoking car, but they didn't care, and had no energy to move.

Max's eyes scanned the station as the train began pulling out. His fear of being followed began to recede. Only the dog had found them. He thought of Griffon being bandaged by the fat, dressing-gown lady.

The dog had given as much as he had gotten. The train's engine was running, and he felt the nearly imperceptible movement as it pulled away from the *quai*.

There. A figure pushing past the others on the escalator, left arm dangling. The scowl! He was there at the station! Griffon looked around savagely, searching. This was the test. He would know the Aix train. If he had recognized them, he would come straight for their train. The cold clutches of fear took Max by surprise as they twisted his stomach again.

The man stamped, turning this way and that, searching the crowd. From inside the train, the dog stared out through the window, alert, silent. The man's eyes roamed, his body moved a step this way, a step that, uncertain. He became smaller, farther away, disappearing with the station as the train moved out from under the enormous glass and lead ceiling into the open air. Max said nothing to Caroline or Nicky. He reached over and patted the dog, which licked his hand in understanding.

Max was right. No one spoke to them during the thirty-five minute trip. Caroline looked out the window in a daze. The horrors of the night began to fade as the train left dismal, crowded apartment buildings behind, and entered the calm, soft world of the French countryside. The sunlight, fresh and new, pierced through clouds to tear away shreds of fear and warm her soul, leaving her sleepy.

Max nudged her out of her dream indicating the tall

smoke stacks of the mining town near their home. Nicky had fallen asleep in his arms and they moved carefully as the train slid to a halt and deposited them on the platform.

'What now?' queried Caroline.

'We start walking.'

18

SOUP, TEA AND CHIPS

'Always butter, chérie. You won't get the flavour right otherwise. Now, remember. As much weight in leeks, carrots, and potatoes. Not quite so many turnips.'

Madame Didier repeated her own soup recipe, insisting on a few lettuce leaves. The pot was now bubbling on the stove and they were just finishing the last of the cleaning up. Madame Didier chattered on about all sorts of things, bathing Fanny's silence in a wash of mundane details. Though she was hardly listening, it was better than being left alone with her black thoughts. Better than being left at the mercy of her own conscience. The doorbell rang.

'*Tu y vas?*' asked Madame Didier in her deep voice. Probably the police back to report that they had found nothing.

'Yes, I'll go,' replied Fanny morosely. She moved slowly to the front door and opened it.

'*Oui?*' she asked, just barely looking up.

'Hi, Fanny. Any tea?'

'Max! Nicky! Caroline!' She stood gawking for a moment, and then the tears bubbled over a tumble of words. Madame Didier, rushing up from behind, enveloped them all in one of her great bear hugs, then flung her solid arms to the heavens.

'*Que le Seigneur soit loué!*' she exclaimed over and over, adding to the babble of incomprehensible questions, half answers, weak yelps from the dog, and plaintive requests from Nicky for food and drink. Finally, when they had all had a warm bath, when Nicky's needs had been seen to; when the dog's paw had been expertly bandaged by Madame Didier, they sat down at the table for a cup of tea that Fanny had prepared. "If only you'd made that tea yesterday afternoon," she chided herself, "none of this would have happened."

'You know, Fanny?' teased Max, squeezing her free hand as she poured his tea, 'I've been waiting a long time for this tea!'

But Fanny pulled her hand from Max's grasp, and turned away, wiping at her eyes with the tea towel.

'Are you crying, Fanny?' Caroline had noticed.

'She's crying for joy that the Lord has kept you all safe,' announced Madame Didier. 'Aren't you, dear?'

Fanny lowered her head, avoiding their eyes. Let them take it as agreement.

Madame Didier made each one of them tell his part of the story in turn. When they got to Fanny, she just said, 'Oh, nothing much happened here, you know. I just sat at home.'

Then they all went round again trying to fit the pieces together.

'I liked the car, and the *pâté*,' Nicky chimed in. The dog, installed at Nicky's feet, seemed to agree, and ran its long tongue around its mouth.

They still couldn't figure out just what the men had been up to, and Max didn't mention the pole that had stopped the Peugeot. Someone suggested that the dog tell its side. Madame Didier assured them that it didn't matter. They were well out of it, that's all.

When the police arrived, they were cross to find the three 'lost' children happily munching biscuits and drinking tea. But their bad humour couldn't dampen the children's high spirits. It was a lovely, happy time. Only Fanny drew aside and busied herself with the dirty dishes. As for the others, their joy spilled over like the tea Fanny poured for Caroline. They were all laughing so hard at Max's description of the fat lady in the lamplight, that in spite of herself, Fanny couldn't help looking up to see his imitation. Suddenly, Caroline shoved her chair back to avoid a hot stream of tea running off the table. They laughed all the harder.

'Fanny, what's the matter with you?' laughed Caroline. 'You know I don't drink tea!' It was true. How had she forgotten?

Fanny was unduly embarrassed. Tears brimmed in her eyes. She knew no one minded anything she did wrong. But *she* still did. They all acted as if it were Christmas, or as if grandparents had come to visit. Conquered, fear and danger had slunk away to let them drink their fill of the cup of joy and laughter, while Fanny still wallowed in despair. 'What's wrong with me?' she asked herself. 'I should be as happy as they all are.'

The familiar sound of their very own diesel Peugeot growled down the driveway. Fanny recognized it before the others. The car was parked at the station. Was Daddy home unexpectedly? Filled with absurd dread at the prospect of seeing him, she slipped unnoticed from the kitchen. A car door slammed and the door flew open. In burst Daddy.

'What's going on here?' he boomed. 'You're not allowed to have all the fun while I'm away!' Max and Caroline exchanged surprised looks and stifled a giggle. Mr Castle gave them no time for questions or explanations.

'Everybody in the car. Quick! We're going to the clinic. You too, Madame Didier.' She turned the soup low, but made no objection. Mr Castle noticed the dog, lying in the corner of the kitchen.

'Who dragged this creature in? Another one of your animal friends, Caroline? But, hey! Where's my birthday girl?'

No one knew where Fanny had gone.

'Get in the car, everybody. I'll nose her out!'

Mr Castle found Fanny lying on her bed, head buried in the pillow.

'Hi, sweetheart. What's up?' He sat down on the bed beside her and stroked her hair. Fanny didn't reply.

'Upset about your birthday, honey? It's all been

most irregular, I must admit!' There was still no answer.

'Fanny.' Mr Castle's voice was firm. 'Turn over and look at me.' Fanny rolled over. 'What is it?'

'I just don't feel too good, Daddy. I don't want to go to the clinic.'

'Nonsense. We're a family, and we're going to the clinic *as* a family. Now stand up and pull yourself together.'

Mr Castle started out of the room. Then he turned back. 'Oh, I nearly forgot! Happy birthday!' He pulled an envelope out of his jacket and laid it on the desk. Then he left. Fanny stood up and pushed a brush through her matted hair. She didn't want to look in the mirror.

The trip was a squash, but no one minded. Dad explained that he'd found a colleague to replace him, and caught the night train home. Max realized that they had probably only missed their dad at the station by an hour or so. He sighed. 'We could have waited at the station...' he murmured.

'We were in the train, too, Daddy,' piped up Nicky.

'Yes, Nicolas, we rode the train last summer.'

'No, Daddy,' insisted Caroline. 'He means just now. This morning.'

'What do you mean, this morning? You just crawled out of bed!'

'And there was a mean man. He grabbed Caroline.'

'What mean man, Nicky?'

'Giffon. I poked him with a driver.'

'Max, what on earth is he talking about? Is this another one of your adventures? I've told you not to get the boy over-excited. He probably had nightmares last night.'

'I don't doubt it, Dad,' answered Max. 'We all did.'

'OK. What's up. What happened?'

Max made a pretty good job of piecing the story together. Fanny sat in dazed silence. Her dad's poem lay tear-stained on her lap. Mr Castle just kept shaking his head in disbelief.

'Well, I'll be,' he interjected from time to time. When Max had finished, he said,

'Now listen, all of you. Your mother will have a fit if you tell her all this. Just let me explain it, when we get to the clinic, OK?'

The clinic visit was much as Fanny had imagined it. The nurses scolded them, just to make a point, but let them all in. Caroline took a picture of them all with her camera, and, having decided that she could love this brand new baby brother just as easily as she had Nicky, excused herself to take some bird pictures in the beautifully wooded grounds of the clinic. Max sat on the edge of his mother's bed rather quiet. He thought his mom looked pretty awful, completely exhausted. But he was extremely tired himself, and felt such genuine peace of mind, that he had no desire to move, or even think. Daddy made light of their adventures, turning them as only he knew how, into one hilarious comedy.

Nicky snuggled into his mother's side, looking

silently at the baby. There was a lull in the conversation.

'I'm here!' shouted Nicky suddenly. They all laughed, but then they just kept on looking at the baby. Mommy displayed Thomas proudly. They all took turns holding him. Finally Mommy turned to Fanny who had been sitting silent in a corner seat after her first polite look at her baby brother.

'Well, dear, tell me what it was like playing mommy for the night. Sounds like you had a rough time of it.'

'It was...' Fanny hesitated. 'Oh, Mommy!' she wailed, and threw herself onto her mother, sobbing uncontrollably. Mrs Castle signalled to her husband with a little thrust of her head. He leaned over her gently and whispered in her ear. She nodded.

'Well, come on you Castle gang,' he announced rather abruptly. 'If I understand it, there's a little shopping to be done, and Madame Didier's soup will burn.' He shooed them all out the door. 'I'll be back for the birthday girl in an hour or so. Bye, my two sweethearts!'

19

EVIDENCE OF THINGS UNSEEN

Fanny cried in long shuddering gasps until the storm of grief subsided, leaving her weary and shaken. Her mother said nothing, but stroked her hair tenderly all the while. When she had been still for some time, baby Thomas began to snuffle in his sheet, and then wail in flat little bleating sounds.

'Fanny,' her mother said kindly, 'just get little Thomas for me please.'

Slowly Fanny stood up, picked a paper hanky out of the box on the bedside table, and blew her nose.

'I'll just wash my hands, first, Mommy,' she said dully, feeling too soiled to touch her perfect new brother. Her face in the mirror as she washed up was a terrible shock. Her fair, freckled skin was horribly splotched from crying, and her hair was a sight. Her lips looked puffy and swollen and drooped dreadfully at the edges. She could feel another cold sore coming. But worst were the eyes. They stared out at her in angry hostility.

'Happy birthday,' she snorted at the hideous image of herself that faced her - an enemy. She stuck out her tongue, then scrubbed cruelly at her face with a wash cloth. But Thomas' crying had become a steady, rhythmic demand by now, and she heard her mother calling.

'Coming, Mom,' she answered, and moved back into the hospital room. Thomas' face was even redder than her own. In fact, it was downright purple. Fanny never had thought that newborn babies were 'cute.' But as she slid one hand under his scrawny neck and the other under his body, she was struck by the tiny, perfect fingers, the downy black hair. Gingerly, cautiously she moved around to the bed, passing him awkwardly to her mother. 'Why does she trust me with him?' thought Fanny. The baby's plaintive cries changed immediately when he felt the soft touch of his mother on his cheek, and his head wobbled hilariously as he searched for a drink. He settled into quick little sucks of satisfaction, punctuated by an occasional rooster-like coo.

Fanny sat beside her mother on the bed, watching in fascination. Mrs Castle's thin legs looked almost spindly on the crisp, white sheet. How strange to see her normal again after months of fat waddling around the house.

'Mommy,' she asked quietly. 'What's it really like to have a baby?'

Her mother stroked Thomas' head with her free hand, looking down at him as if searching for her answer in his miraculous presence. After long seconds she spoke.

'It's the most wonderful, frightening, overwhelming, miraculous experience a person can ever have. And rather difficult to describe, what's more,' her mother smiled.

Fanny remained silent. There didn't seem much to say.

'How can I explain it?' went on her mother. 'Yesterday I left you and came in here. Daddy has always been with me before. This time I was alone.' Fanny watched her mother's eyes glaze over as she re-lived the memories of the previous day. 'Things didn't go too well, really,' she sighed, hesitant to say more.

'What happened, Mommy?' urged Fanny, curious. Then, sensing her mother's hesitation she added, 'But, if you don't want to talk about it, I understand.'

'It was fine at the beginning. Just like the others. I don't ever mind the pain, in a way. I've always thought that the more intense it is, the quicker the baby comes. So usually I cheer it on.'

Fanny felt her mother's arm slide around her shoulders, and she lay her head against Mrs Castle, while toying with Thomas' miniature toes.

'But Thomas got stuck. Turned sideways. It went on for hours and hours.' Her mother spoke to her as an equal, a friend. Fanny listened, silent.

'It was a black pit, and I was in it all alone. I had no more strength, no control. Even the Lord seemed far away.' Mrs Castle sat silent. Baby Thomas began to doze.

'I suppose the loneliness was the worst. There was no way out but through, and I had to do it alone. No one could reach in and help me.'

Her mother's honesty made Fanny suddenly bold.

'Not even God?' she asked, hardly daring more than a whisper.

Mrs Castle looked sharply at her daughter. But Fanny's face was lowered, and she could read nothing of her meaning. She paused, then answered with a sigh of admission, 'No, love. Not even God. At least that's what it seemed to me.'

'Is the Lord upset with you, then? Angry?'

'He would have every right to be,' replied Mrs. Charles softly. 'I've certainly had enough years to learn to trust Him!' She smiled. 'But no. He forgives us. If we are His children, we don't have to fear God's anger - Jesus took all that when he died for us. All God sees when He looks at us is the beauty of Jesus.'

Fanny watched her brother lying in total peace, asleep, his head rolling back on his mother's arm. The three of them sat noiseless in the warm morning sun. Then Fanny felt her mother's arm squeeze her shoulder.

'Daddy should be back soon,' said Mrs Castle. 'And I've been thoughtless, talking only about myself. What about you, darling? Did you want to talk about last night?'

Fanny smiled.

'We just did,' she replied mysteriously, and would say no more.

20

BIRDS OF ANOTHER KIND

And so it might have ended but for one fact. Caroline had little time to prepare her bird report. Things were hectic at home with Mom gone. They'd managed a lovely birthday for Fanny in the end, with a beautifully decorated cake that the neighbourhood *patisserie* had offered completely free when they found out that it was for Fanny *and* Thomas Castle. Dad didn't have time to get the pictures developed. But Caroline insisted, and Nicky desperately wanted a dog bowl for Chips.

Daddy went out himself on Monday night to a one-hour photo shop, and Caroline got up early Tuesday morning to glue them into her report. Max helped her, as he had promised.

There was a good picture of the family, which Max thought the teacher might like to see. She had one of a magpie and one of a swallow from the clinic. But in the middle of the photos there was one she didn't remember taking. It was crooked and there were four pigeons in the foreground.

'Hey, let me see that one,' insisted Max, in an excited voice. 'Where did you take that?'

'I didn't,' she replied. 'I don't know who did.'

'I'll bet I know.'

'Who do you think?'

'Nicky,' stated Max.

'Nicky?' she asked incredulously.

'Yup. Look at the way it's taken - all crooked, and look there in the background. Don't you remember that place?' Caroline examined the picture more closely. It did look familiar somehow. The courtyard!

'But who are those two men, then?'

'What? You don't recognize that one on the left?' It dawned on Max that he had seen a lot more of Monsieur Griffon's face than Caroline had. 'Well that's our friendly neighbour, of course, and the other fellow, I don't know. What did she yell, that lady? Did you hear her?'

'I can't remember any of that. I was just hiding as far down in the back seat as I could.' Max made her give him the picture, even though the pigeons were not bad at all.

It might even have ended there, were it not for the laundry. Fanny took some time to catch up on all the dirty laundry while her mom was in the clinic. She had her own school work to do, and there were plenty of other chores. It wasn't until Tuesday evening that she finally found Nicky's trousers and the great woolly jacket in a heap upstairs in the bathroom cupboard.

Chips, who followed anyone around the house, unless Nicky was available, cringed when she walked past him with the knit jacket. She sorted the colours and went through the pockets before washing anything. She knew better than to throw away any precious drawings and documents from Nicky or Caroline, and unfolded the papers in Nicky's trousers with great care. She saw her brother's familiar little men, but more interesting were the documents that had served him as scrap paper. On them were recorded detailed transactions that seemed to be ownership papers of some kind. There were plenty of numbers and weights marked in various places. She showed them to Max, who became very excited.

They found and examined still other papers from the woolly jacket. On these were financial accounts. Max stopped by the mayor's office that evening. They sent him to the *gendarmerie*. A gruff, elderly officer took the papers and listened stone-faced to Max's somewhat vague explanations. He almost regretted having come. Now he was obliged to turn over these precious documents to the police, though he had taken the precaution of photocopying them at school that day.

Caroline gave her report at school. Fanny left a note in the neighbour's mailbox asking if they wanted their dog back, but she never received a reply. Mrs Griffon moved away to be with her family in Bordeaux. Chips was there to stay. He followed Nicky like a shadow, and lay outside the school gate all day, waiting. His limp was pronounced and would never heal properly, but no one seemed to mind. How Nicky came to choose the name Chips for the dog, no one ever knew, but Caroline was delighted.

Thomas Ronald came home to rule his new kingdom. Fanny worked hard. Nicky was unlike himself, and Max went back to life as usual. His mo-ped had been returned. Three weeks later, however, Daddy received a phone call from the *gendarmerie* informing him that his son Max was to receive a reward for having contributed valuable information leading to the arrest of two car thieves. Max had been exactly right. Monsieur Griffon and his friends had been collecting stolen cars, or cars that had been in accidents. They would 'cut' off the bad parts and 'paste' the good bits together to make 'new' cars. Max felt obliged to share his reward five ways. He bought himself a new watch. Nicky bought the fanciest dog collar he could find and wanted Chips' name engraved on it, with his own underneath. Caroline chose an enormous drawing kit, and bought a bag of potato chips, which she left unopened on her desk for years. Thomas Ronald's money went into a piggy bank until he was old enough to decide how to spend it.

As for Fanny, she bought a lovely framed picture of a sleeping baby to put over Thomas' bed. On the back she wrote in her best calligraphy, "May 15: I will lie down and sleep in peace, for you alone, O Lord, make me dwell in safety."

GLOSSARY

French / English

GLOSSARY

French / English

Griffon: A family name, but which resembles the word for claw (griffe).

Sainte Victoire: The famous mountain that dominates the countryside near Aix-en-Provence and was painted by such famous people as Cézanne, and Winston Churchill.

Cézanne: A famous nineteenth century French painter who lived and worked in Aix-en-Provence for many years.

allô: Hello (for the telephone only).

viens ici, gros chien! C'est mon ballon: Come here, big doggie! That's my ball.

Ou es-tu? J'ai peur: Where are you? I'm scared!

Vinaigrette: French salad dressing, made with oil, vinegar, salt and pepper.

FR 13: French licence plates identify the département in the last two numbers.

les Bouches du Rhône: One of the 95 'départements' in France.

département: These are like American states, but do not have as much independence in creating and applying their own laws.

vieux port: old port, dating back to the first century. There is an even older one, a few hundred yards further inland, recently uncovered, which dates back to the Phoenicians (7th century B.C.)

Je dois faire pipi: I need the toilet.

allée du Lavoir: Washing alley.

Corsica: A spectacularly beautiful Mediterranean island off the coast of France to the southeast of Marseille.

Chateau d'If: A tiny island about a twenty minute boat ride from Marseille. It was used as a prison, and held some Huguenot pastors as well as criminals.

Oui, maman va bien: Yes, Mommy's fine.

Qu'est-ce que tu as, ma grande?: What's the matter, big girl?

A vrai dire: To tell the truth.

mamie: Grandma.

peuchère: an amusing slang interjection common in provence.

gendarmerie: police station.

un instant: one moment.

pas possible: impossible.

quartier résidentiel: residential neighbourhood.

Excusez-moi, madame: Pardon me, ma'am.

Gauloises: A famous brand of French cigarettes.

Connais pas: Don't know.

Callanques: The rocky shores to the west of Marseille.

restaurant: The name of a large loaf of bread in the same shape as a *baguette* (long and thin - the word means 'wand') but larger.

Allez, viens. On va faire de la soupe toi et moi: We're going to make soup, you and I.

corniche: in this case, the ridge of land which follows the coast around Marseille.

Je veux du pain: I want some bread.

Espèce de crétin: 'You idiot!' (colloquial slang).

Vite! C'est Kaffi!: Quick! It's Kaffi.

pâté: a delicate paste.

Va-t-en, méchant: Go away, meanie.

Arrête: stop

C'est honteux: It's disgraceful!

La Canebière: The main avenue which runs through Marseille, and meets the old port.

sale gamine: dirty kid (colloquial slang).

Aix: (pronounced 'ex') short for Aix-en-Provence, a town which goes back to pre-Roman times. Aix lies about 18 miles north of Marseille.

contrôleur: ticket collector.

Marseille to **Gardanne**: Gardanne is a small mining town to the south of Aix, and the last stop on the train line before Aix.

quai: platform.

Chérie: dear.

Tu y vas?: Are you going?

Que le Seigneur soit loué: The Lord be praised!

patisserie: bakery (especially for cakes).

Bordeaux: A large town on the southwest coast of France.